# CAPTAIN CHARLES RAWN
## AND THE
# FRONTIER INFANTRY
## IN MONTANA

# CAPTAIN CHARLES RAWN AND THE FRONTIER INFANTRY IN MONTANA

ROBERT M. BROWN, PhD

*Foreword by Gary Glynn*

Published by The History Press
Charleston, SC
www.historypress.net



*Front cover, top*: Original artwork by Bryan Steward, artist; *bottom*: Dress parade at Fort Missoula, from the collection of Stan Cohen.

First published 2016

ISBN 9781531698751

Library of Congress Control Number: 2016932972

*Notice*: The information in this book is true and complete to the best of our knowledge. It is offered without guarantee on the part of the author or The History Press. The author and The History Press disclaim all liability in connection with the use of this book.

*This work is dedicated to Claudia:*
*my wife, soul mate, best friend—the love of my life. You make it all possible.*

# CONTENTS

# FOREWORD

I first encountered Captain Charles Rawn on a fine spring day at the site of Fort Fizzle, scene of a confrontation in Montana's Lolo Canyon between hundreds of Nez Perce warriors and a small contingent of US Army soldiers and local civilians.

Dressed in an impeccable blue uniform trimmed with gold braid, wearing a black campaign hat and armed with a single-action pistol, Captain Rawn cut an imposing figure as he described the events of the 1877 Nez Perce War to a group of local schoolchildren. They listened raptly as Rawn described his role as leader of the small force at Fort Fizzle and told of his unsuccessful attempts to negotiate a peaceful surrender with the Nez Perce leaders, including Looking Glass, White Bird and Joseph.

Most of the schoolchildren who learned the story of Fort Fizzle from Captain Rawn never realized that the uniformed figure who portrayed Rawn was in fact Dr. Robert M. Brown, the executive director of the Historical Museum at Fort Missoula.

Rawn was the founder and first commander of Fort Missoula, and Dr. Brown spent years researching his historic alter ego, making him uniquely qualified to write the story of one of the little-known but important figures of the frontier army.

Whole bookshelves have been filled with biographies of a few prominent soldiers who fought the Indian wars, in particular Lieutenant Colonel George A. Custer, who famously lost his entire battalion after a rash attack on a vastly superior force. On the other hand, there has been little written of the everyday lives of the mid-level officers of the frontier army, those men who were focused on doing their jobs and keeping their men alive rather than seeking fame and promotion.

Rawn was raised in an upper-middle-class family in Pennsylvania yet chose a career that would take him away from the comforts of civilization for years at a time. He and his family would spend most of their lives in a nearly lawless land where a small number of soldiers were tasked with keeping an uneasy peace between newly arrived settlers and the Native Americans who had occupied the land for millennia.

It is telling that when the US Army drastically downsized at the end of the Civil War, many well-regarded officers were mustered out of service. Rawn, on the other hand, was not only retained as an officer but also kept his wartime rank of captain while many of his peers faced major reductions in rank. Rawn's story provides insight into the hardships experienced by those who chose a career in the postwar military, which for most officers proved a thankless job with little chance for advancement and was often characterized by a frustrating series of postings to remote forts.

Who were these men who chose to serve their country for little pay or recognition? What motivated them to remain as career military officers despite harsh living conditions? In *Captain Charles Rawn and the Frontier Infantry in Montana*, Dr. Brown has given us a rare and long overdue insight into the day-to-day lives of the front-line officers who were the backbone of the frontier army during the last half of the nineteenth century.

—Gary Glynn
author of *That Beautiful Little Post: The Story of Fort Missoula*

# ACKNOWLEDGEMENTS

Writing this book has been a labor of love, and I wish to thank all those whose help and encouragement made it possible. First, a huge thank-you to my wife, Claudia, for all of her support and encouragement; to Jennifer Steward, my in-house IT and photograph expert; and to artist Bryan Steward for his tremendous cover art and maps. Thank you to Gary Glynn, John Rimel, Stan Cohen, Rickard Ross, David Eckroth and Minie Smith for their counsel and advice. I am incredibly grateful for the help that I received from the Historical Museum at Fort Missoula, especially that of colleague and friend, curator Nicole Webb. Ken Frew, research librarian, and Janet Bowen, curator, at the Historical Society of Dauphin County in Harrisburg, Pennsylvania, were unfailing in providing help going through their extraordinary collection of Rawn family material and local photographs. I could not have done this without the assistance of Rachel Phillips, research coordinator at Bozeman's Gallatin History Museum, and Leslie Lulu at the Big Hole National Battlefield, as they guided me through their valuable research files. The assistance of the staffs at the Montana Historical Society's Research Library, Pennsylvania State Library, D'Arcy McNickle Library at Salish Kootenai College and retired archivist Dale Johnson and the staff at the Mike and Maureen Mansfield Library at the University of Montana were invaluable. Finally, a big thank-you to Bob Beatty, chief operating officer of the American Association for State and Local History, for suggesting this project in the first place; and to Artie Crisp at The History Press for his guidance. I am incredibly appreciative of all of your assistance. Naturally, all errors are my own and no one else's.

# INTRODUCTION

I first became acquainted with Captain Charles Rawn in 1991, when I became executive director of the Historical Museum at Fort Missoula. As founder of Fort Missoula, Rawn made an enticing study, and the more I studied him, the more I realized what his career meant on the bigger stage of the frontier army in Montana. Captain Rawn was no General Sheridan, no General Howard, no Colonel Miles, and he certainly was no Colonel Custer. Captain Rawn was an ordinary man. He created no legacy and he left no statues behind; he just did what he had to do for reasons that were known largely only to himself.

He was born in extremely turbulent times, an era of two major, violent cultural clashes. He grew up during the period of rising animosity between the free North and the increasingly belligerent slaveholding South. Yet he undoubtedly learned tolerance and empathy for the downtrodden on his many walks with his abolitionist father along the Susquehanna River in Harrisburg, Pennsylvania. When the Civil War broke out, he quickly enlisted to do his part, and he served ably but without distinction throughout the course of the Civil War and Reconstruction, rising to the rank of captain in the 7$^{th}$ US Infantry by the end of the war.

With the embers of the Civil War and Reconstruction still smoldering, Captain Rawn found himself thrown immediately into a new and very different kind of cultural war. The Civil War could be understood by both parties in similar words and thoughts; they shared a common history, similar religious belief systems, mutual philosophies and a world view (despite some very different interpretations). Before, during and after the War of the Rebellion, men on opposing sides could and did understand one another; they even frequently respected their opponents for their beliefs and sacrifices. However, the conflict that Captain Rawn found himself facing in the West was vastly different, and neither side could understand the attitudes or thought processes of the other. There was no commonality of history, religion, philosophy or world view, and they defined each other in very disparaging and racist terms. These two cultures would not and could not coexist. Captain Rawn found himself in a situation where the cultures were already at war, and the army was not prepared. But ready or not, the army was already participating in the pacification of the West and the subjugation of Indians.

It is tempting to address the issue of the Indian Wars in a stark, black-and-white manner, and indeed this was the way most people interpreted it at the time. Still, it must be remembered that there were many tribes, including the Salish, Crow, Mandan, Chippewa, Ojibwe and even the Nez Perce before 1877, that coexisted relatively peacefully with the white settlers over long periods of time. Even these, however, had to eventually adapt to the white man's culture to survive. Instead of a black-and-white story, this is a history with many shades of gray and with shifting allegiances on both sides over time, in which Captain Rawn played a significant and instructive, if minor, role.

General William T. Sherman, general of the US Army throughout most of this time period, clearly defined the issue from the typical white man's perspective when he described the Indians as simply savages who had to be displaced by the irresistible progress of the white race—by western civilization's Manifest Destiny. The Indians, if they could not adapt, simply had to be removed, isolated or destroyed so that white civilization could rightfully advance and the United States could reach its full potential. As the *Weekly Missoulian* stated on June 29, 1877, with the Nez Perce rampaging across Idaho, "the government must either protect her pioneer citizens and property or surrender the fields of the Northwest to the domination of the savage." To most whites, the Indians were considered simply inferior; as the *Weekly Missoulian* stated on August 10, 1877, before it became aware of the disaster at the Battle of the Big Hole, "The Indians are simply homeless children, growing up in ignorance, idleness and vice." They did not belong in the white man's world.

On the other hand, the Indians, the army's opponents on the frontier, saw the white man as naturally inferior to themselves. These Native Americans had lived on the land and loved the land for centuries before the white man arrived with his strange ways. There was no commonality of attitude, no shared experiences and no comprehension of the different value systems. The Indians viewed themselves as special; most tribal names when translated from the original Indian language refer to each indigenous Native American tribe as "the people." The "others" were different, strange and inferior, and they had to be dealt with appropriately.

With such exalted self-images, neither side had any incentive to adapt or learn about the other; their way was the only way. To each side, the other was not only different culturally, but they also all looked alike, creating a perpetual underlying theme of racism, mistrust and indiscriminating hate. After all, if "they" all looked alike, it was acceptable to punish any and all available "enemy." This is why the US Army could attack and destroy entire villages of innocent Indians and why Indian raiding parties could attack innocent men, women and children on the frontier. This was a war of two cultures that could not coexist—it was a war to the death.

This attitude permeated the mindsets of the men and women of both sides. For Captain Rawn, as part of the army, the instrument of American culture, it went even deeper. The written and spoken words of the leaders of the army, government and society filtered down to the average soldier. American expansion was God-ordained, and the army was the vanguard and protector of that white male civilization. Those in the way were brutal heathens and savages. They were subhuman. The fact that the Indians had a mystical and incomprehensible culture only made them seem nonsensical and more contemptible. There could be no mercy; there could be only total effort for the "right" way. Indian policy, as complicated as it might have seemed, was actually very simple: annihilation or assimilation. But it would take the frontier army a very long time to accomplish it.

Charles C. Rawn lived through it all and played major roles in several important actions. His career provides us with a window to look at the growing pains of an America coming to grips with very important and divisive issues. Growing up with an abolitionist father and learning to feel empathy for the enslaved, he quickly entered the Union army in 1861. His career during the Civil War was mostly administrative, but he played an active role in some unfortunate episodes during Reconstruction that would color his outlook on those less fortunate. In the West, as senior captain of the 7th Infantry, Rawn participated in both the Sioux War and the Nez Perce War. He was instrumental in staving off defeat at the Battle of Pryor's Creek against Sitting Bull's forces, and he played an integral role during the flight of the Nez Perce through western Montana, particularly at Lolo Canyon and at the Battle of the Big Hole.

By studying Captain Rawn's personality and military career during the Civil War, Reconstruction and on the frontier, it is possible to better understand the nature of life in the regular army and the hardship of life in the frontier West. How did the army transform itself from a million-man battering ram during the Civil War to what became, eventually, an elite strike force in the West? How did the men react? How did the soldiers and their families survive the hardships inherent in duty on the frontier? How did technology turn the tide? How did leadership evolve? And how did men like Charles Rawn survive, learn and adapt to their hostile environments?

Following and understanding Charles Rawn's career with the 7th Infantry, and particularly his career in frontier Montana (1872–79), can help us answer these questions. His adventures and duties while on the frontier portray him as a man trusted by his superiors and admired by his subordinates. As reported in the *Weekly Missoulian*, after the Battle of the Big Hole, "Capt. Rawn is deserving of especial mention for his bravery and coolness in the presence of appalling danger. After his chief was wounded the direction of affairs largely devolved on him, and it was grand to witness the readiness in which the men followed where he went and their confidence in his leadership."

As a man doing his best in trying situations, he proved his worth both in combat and on routine post duty. Although he was an unheralded, minor player on a huge stage, it is exactly men like Captain Charles C. Rawn who "won" the West.

CHAPTER 1

# THE EARLY YEARS

Charles Coatesworth Rawn was born in Harrisburg, Pennsylvania, on December 6, 1837, to upper-middle-class parents: Charles Coatesworth Pinckney Rawn and Frances Peacock Clendenin Rawn. He was the third of seven children but the first one to reach maturity. A first child was stillborn; the second, Elizabeth, was born with a spinal disorder and died in infancy after Charles's birth. Two other siblings died in infancy, and two survived to adulthood: Frances Clendenin Rawn and John Calvin Rawn.

Young Charles grew up in a comfortable setting but in uncomfortable times, as the ever-increasing tensions between the northern and southern states eventually culminated in the Civil War. His father was well connected and influential and had great influence over the upbringing of his son. Charles Sr. was born on July 30, 1802, to David and Elizabeth Rawn in Georgetown, Washington, D.C. His grandparents were German natives, Caspar and Barbara Rahn (original spelling). In 1808, his father died and his mother moved to Delaware City, Pennsylvania. He graduated from West Chester Academy in 1826 and relocated to Harrisburg, where he apprenticed with his cousin Francis Shunk, who was elected governor in 1844. He was admitted to the bar in 1831, and in 1833, he married eighteen-year-old Frances Peacock Clendenin of Harrisburg. They lived in Market Square in the center of Harrisburg, a short walk from the Susquehanna River where he would take many walks with his young son.

Charles Coatesworth Pinckney Rawn left behind twenty-nine journals, from February 20, 1830, to December 18, 1865; they are now located at the

Historical Society of Dauphin County, in Harrisburg, Pennsylvania. These volumes address the weather, his personal and professional activities and many financial transactions. It is through these journals that he emerges as methodical and objective, sentimental and moralistic—a man devoted to his profession but also a dutiful father. He was a devout man and was one of the original seven trustees of the Presbyterian Church of Harrisburg, at Chestnut and Second, organized in 1859, although he also attended Front Street Episcopalian Church with his mother-in-law. When neither of these was available, he attended services in local Baptist, Reformed and Lutheran churches. Attendance at church for Charles Sr., as well as for most Americans at the time, provided not only worship but also fellowship and entertainment. It was natural that his children also attended church; it was expected.

Charles Coatesworth Pinckney Rawn (1802–1865), attorney and leading abolitionist in Harrisburg, Pennsylvania, the father of Charles Coatesworth Rawn; no date. *Courtesy Historical Society of Dauphin County, Harrisburg, Pennsylvania.*

He set up his law office at 7 South Second at Market Street, close to his home and the center of activity of the capital city. He quickly gained a reputation as a criminal defense specialist, although he occasionally acted as prosecutor. Charging two to ten dollars at first, he later increased his fees to fifty dollars for a case. He was active in the community as a Mason (as would be his son) and closely followed the activities of the anti-Masons. He served as deputy attorney general for Dauphin County in 1833 and was a member of the Pennsylvania Canal Commission, Harrisburg Library Association and school board. He invested in local banks and manufacturing companies. He was a leader of the local militia, and during the Civil War, Secretary of War Edwin Stanton appointed him the commissioner of the board of enrollment for the Fourteenth Congressional District. In his journals, Charles mentioned many of the influential men with whom he mingled: Andrew Jackson, Martin Van Buren, Nicolas Biddle, Henry Clay, Daniel Webster, John C. Calhoun, William Lloyd Garrison, Frederick Douglass, Ralph Waldo Emerson and Abraham Lincoln. He was also an active supporter and associate

Market Square, Harrisburg, Pennsylvania, with the Presbyterian church in the center, circa 1883. This is the immediate area where the Rawns lived and the church they attended. From *Photographic Wanderings Around Harrisburg*, by A.M. Allen, Pottsville, Pennsylvania. *Courtesy Historical Society of Dauphin County, Harrisburg, Pennsylvania.*

of fellow Pennsylvanian James Buchanan and considered himself a Free Soil Democrat.

He was an earnest opponent of human slavery, although his attitude toward blacks was complicated. During the days of the Fugitive Slave Law, he was an eloquent pleader on behalf of poor blacks. His journal is full of the mention of many African American clients, workers and household employees. He also defended black rioters and runaways in the Harrisburg courts. But his racial attitudes were complicated, as they were for many Americans at the time; nor were they always generous. For example, he was careful to keep track of race in his journals, referring to colored, black, mixed-race yellow and Irishmen. In 1837, he signed a letter in support of settling freed blacks in Liberia; in 1842, he condemned a black workman for "rascally" extorting his sister into paying too much for hauling a trunk, stating that the man was a "nigger"; and in 1843, he angrily pursued one of his own black servants who had run away. However, these attitudinal contradictions were prevalent throughout white society, north and south.

But his attitude hardened after 1850. It was the Federal Fugitive Slave Act that propelled Charles deeper into the depths of the "peculiar institution" and one case in particular. James Philips, a black resident of Harrisburg, was arrested in June 1852 as the escaped slave of Henry Fant of Virginia. The witnesses for Fant admitted that the escaped slave had been gone for fifteen or sixteen years and that he had been only eleven or twelve years old when he ran away. The only positive identification they could provide was that Philips bore a family resemblance to the slaves still in bondage to Fant. Federal slave commissioner Richard McAllister, presiding over the case, ruled against Philips and produced a writ already filled out to return the man to his rightful master. The next day, slave catchers took him to Richmond, where they sold him to a slave dealer for $505. The shock of seeing a long-term resident of Harrisburg brutally committed to slavery spurred several local men to raise money to buy his freedom. Charles C.P. Rawn was chosen to travel to Richmond on the mission of mercy to procure Philips's freedom. He wrote in shock and despair of his experiences in Virginia, his words representing a matter-of-fact yet harsh indictment of the system. On July 10, 1852, he wrote:

> *While looking round I witnessed the most horrible, and Heaven defying scenes of the inspection & sale of 5 or 6 females ranging from 17 to 26 or 30 years old, 3 of them with infant children...another stout strong looking man 40 to 44 yrs old all put up "warranted sound" and title perfect... The man was taken behind a screen, his trowsers stripped down to his feet and his shirt pushed on to his waist as though his private parts, behind & spine and thighs and legs were the parts most desirable to be perfect...He was put on the "block" as they call it, being something like a large table or platform abt 6 ft by 4 mounted by 4 to 5 steps where the slave stands while the auctioneer sells him...*
>
> *They are carefully examined by the hardened looking dealers who appeared there in numbers from 50 to 100...one female was taken behind the screen for more special examination—several men going and any one that chose to, to look at her. They undid some part of her dress about the*

> *shoulders & chest. I understand since that this is frequently for the purpose of examining their backs, shoulders &c to see if they have been much injured by whipping.*[1]

That this made such a tremendous impact on the Harrisburg lawyer cannot be denied, and one can imagine Charles Sr. imparting his feelings of disgust and rage to his young son in words similar to those he wrote in his diary:

> *The more I see however the More I detest & abhor the accursed business. That it is accursed of Heaven I as firmly believe as that I believe in the Justice and goodness of God. And this Nation will yet weep over this National sin of slavery & a slave trade in sackcloth & ashes and the severer Judgment of a righteous God who will surely visit us as a Nation with our National sins.*[2]

On normal days, he walked for an hour a day in good weather, often mentioning doing so with his son "Chas." Later, after Charles moved away to school, he continued his walks with his youngest son, John Calvin (1846–1926). He took his family on carriage rides, indulged in gardening and attended temperance meetings but enjoyed a drink or two with his friends and colleagues. He gambled on elections, attended the theater and played quoits (a game similar to horseshoes), except on Sundays. When he died, someone (not his son Charles, according to handwriting comparisons) wrote at the end of the journal: "The faithful hand here ceased its labours, laid down its pen, never to resume it, and after a brief struggle with the king of terrors, calmly fell asleep in Jesus on the morning of the 18th of Dec 1865. Let me die the death of the righteous and let my last end be like his." He was a good man, and his son learned much under his tutelage.

Charles's journal entry for December 6, 1837, states very simply that he arose at 4:30 a.m. and "went for Dr. Wm. Rutherford for my wife who gave birth to a very fine large son at about 7½ a.m." This young boy was named Charles Coatesworth Rawn, and his father's journals reflect a close and caring relationship between the two of them. Charles Sr. wrote about their walks, usually of four miles or more. He took his son shooting, on visits to clients and to church with his wife, and he included occasional comments on young Charles's schooling, such as the November 24, 1853 entry: "Chas also home at supper—Chas went to his teachers, Mr. Demarests at 6¾ PM to review his Latin." They also had moments of fun, as when he took his son to a horse race and bought him some ground nuts on August 4, 1851, or the following week when the two of them went to Cape May, New Jersey, where he wrote that they "took to the surf in our buff at 5½ a.m." After his eldest son went away to preparatory school and then Princeton, the journals make reference to sending his son letters and newspapers. These references to letters sent to his son continue almost up to his death in 1865.

One can imagine young Charles, at the side of his father, trying to keep up and listening intently to his father as they walked along the Susquehanna River or down to the courthouse. His father would talk about what was going on in Harrisburg and beyond, imbuing his son with a sense of being alive during important and challenging times, with a sense of purpose and duty and with a sense of empathy for those less fortunate. They would discuss politics, both local and national, and lament the failure of the Democratic Party to respond to the expansion of slavery. They would talk about the Mexican War and what it meant for the future of slavery and the frontier. His father would have talked to his son about his visit to the Richmond slave market. Discussions would focus on the Compromise of 1850, the passage of the Kansas-Nebraska Act and the repeal of the Missouri Compromise of 1820 and the resulting disaster that was Bleeding Kansas. The stories of the efforts of William Lloyd Garrison, Frederick Douglass, Harriot Tubman, the abolitionists and the Underground Railroad must have made an impact on the impressionable boy. Later, when young Charles went away to school, the stories of John Brown at Pottawatomie Creek in Kansas in 1856, followed by Brown's stirring raid on the US arsenal at Harpers Ferry, Virginia, in 1859 and, finally, the presidential election of 1860 and the resulting villainous actions of the Southern secessionists would have filled his father's letters. Young Charles would have learned well the evils of slavery and developed a firm commitment to do something about it, to make the United States a better nation in the image of his father. If his chosen way to meet the challenge—enlisting in the army—was not his father's preferred response, his father understood and supported that decision. The fact that Charles Sr. would live long enough to see the end of the evil institution of slavery, and knowing that his son had played a role in that result, must have meant a great deal to young Charles.

Charles Jr. also learned to keep his own daily journal; unfortunately, he kept one only for part of 1856, when he attended Tremont Seminary in Norristown, Pennsylvania. While living at this preparatory school and visiting home occasionally, Charles learned his Latin lessons daily and his German lessons on Mondays, Wednesdays and Fridays. While there were

*Left*: Abolitionist John Brown (1800–1859), 1859. In opposition to the pacifist abolitionist movement, Brown advocated violence, and his 1859 raid on the federal arsenal at Harpers Ferry led to increased tension between the North and South. *Courtesy Library of Congress*.

*Below*: The Harrisburg Capitol area where Charles Coatesworth Pinckney Rawn worked, circa 1880. View looking west to State Street from the Capitol, with a Civil War monument in the middle of Second Street and Grace United Methodist Church and St. Patrick's Cathedral on the right. *Courtesy Historical Society of Dauphin County, Harrisburg, Pennsylvania*.

no Greek lessons available at the time, he did take French. He referenced studying geometry, algebra, chemistry and physiology. He noted that he played the violin at times and smoked the occasional cigar. He wrote about sleighing almost every day in January and about freezing his feet off and on and a lot about foot pain. In fact, he was not a particularly healthy young man and would never be a particularly healthy adult. In 1856, he was sick the last two days of February and the entire month of March. He was sick again on April 18–27, May 6–12 and May 28–29. He wrote that he had a cold in January and mumps in February and mentioned wanting to take only homeopathic medicine. He saw a German homeopathic physician beginning in March, which apparently did not do much good. During March, he wrote that he had a chill and that the chill came on him only at certain times of the day; but on March 20, he noted that he had been throwing up blood. At that point, staying in the nursing room, he finally had a regular doctor take care of him, and he started to feel better after a while.

Meanwhile, when he was not sick, he managed to attend an antislavery lecture by Senator Giddings of Ohio on April 4. His father visited him in April, bringing with him his summer clothes. His mother visited him on May 10, and he accompanied her by train to Philadelphia before returning to school. On June 5, he left school and took the train home to Harrisburg. On June 18, his father told him that he was going to go to Edgehill Grammar School in Princeton, New Jersey. He left for Princeton on June 24 and checked in at the school on June 26, mentioning that he would not see his father for three months.

Entering Princeton as a sophomore, Charles kept a lesson book, also housed at the Historical Society of Dauphin County. His notes of the lectures are typical for the time period. There were lectures on philosophy; metaphysical science; physics; algebra; space, duration and matter; measurements; and the property of matter, metals and gases. There are handwritten copies of "Odes of Horace," "The Second Book of the Orders of Horace," "The Exodus of Horace," "Odes to Maecenas," "To Augustus Caesar," "To Virgil" and others. Upon the subject of "Truth," he commented that "Truth" was a "great term that includes all objects of study…This is a term too valuable to be misunderstood—One cannot define it. We can only characterize it. Its great characteristic is <u>consistency with some great standard</u>." He was his father's son.

Interestingly, and unexpectedly, on the inside back cover of Charles's 1858 lesson book are military notes. These include the "Manual of Musket," with copied notes on shoulder arms, support arms, carry arms, present arms,

View of Nassau Hall, Princeton, New Jersey, where Charles Rawn attended college, 1860. *Courtesy Library of Congress.*

etc. There are descriptions on how to load, charge, draw a rammer, ram a cartridge, return, ram, ready, aim and fire. There are also instructions on how to load in two motions; detailed diagrams of two platoons, with locations noted for the captain, first lieutenant and second lieutenant; and the relationship to the battalion is remarked upon. Obviously, young Charles's mind had an unexpected military bent. It would not be too long until he answered the call to arms and to his future.

CHAPTER 2

# CIVIL WAR AND RECONSTRUCTION

At 4:30 a.m. on April 12, 1861, General P.G.T. Beauregard's forces of the newly formed Confederate States of America opened fire on the Federal forces garrisoning Fort Sumter in Charleston Harbor, South Carolina. The next day, Union major Robert Anderson agreed to surrender the fortress, and on April 15, President Lincoln issued a call for seventy-five thousand volunteers to serve ninety-day enlistments to put down the rebellion.

On May 2, Charles C. Rawn volunteered as a private in the newly formed Company F of the 25th Infantry, part of the Pennsylvania Volunteers, or "Lochiel Grays." This did not please his father, who wrote in his journal entry for July 25, "I did not wish myself that Chas should enter the Army at all, nor did I feel entirely free to dissuade him from it." However, one wonders if Charles Sr. was not secretly proud that his son had volunteered in the war to eliminate slavery from the country. The journals show that Charles Sr. closely followed the course of the Civil War. For example, on July 16, he toured the battleground near Hagerstown, Maryland; he visited Washington, D.C., on July 20 and listened to President Lincoln; and on July 23, he learned that "our boys," the Lochiel Grays, were at Harpers Ferry, Virginia, and that his son had been unwell with a cold, fever and toothache.

On July 25, Charles Sr. was at the Willards Hotel in Washington, D.C., where he was informed by a friend that the secretary of war, Simon Cameron, had expressed a desire to give his son a lieutenant's commission

The old Pennsylvania Railroad Station (1857–87), from which thousands of Pennsylvanian volunteers left to serve in the Civil War, 1863. *Courtesy Historical Society of Dauphin County, Harrisburg, Pennsylvania.*

in the regular army. It is worth noting that Cameron succeeded James Buchanan as US senator for Pennsylvania and was a contender for the Republican Party's nomination for president in 1860 before serving as Lincoln's secretary of war for one year and then resigning due to corruption; one suspects that Charles Sr. was one of his staunch supporters to have that kind of favor granted presumably without having asked for it. In that same day's journal entry, he wrote "that Chas had expressed himself to me as preferring the artillery arm of the service if he did enter." Obviously his son was not happy as a private in the infantry. The following day, at a meeting at the War Department, Charles Sr. learned that his son was indeed to be commissioned a second lieutenant, but in the $7^{th}$ Infantry, not the artillery.

Charles Sr. followed his son's career throughout the war, dutifully noting in his journal writing and receiving letters from his son's postings from New Mexico to New York. In one particular entry, on December 6, 1863, his feelings for his son come through more than at any other point as he wrote and underscored, "This is our son <u>Charles Birth day ~ He is 26 Years old.</u>" On June 26, 1864, he wrote, with evident great relief, "We received

Secretary of War Simon Cameron (1799–1889), 1861. After making his fortune in railroads and banking, Cameron entered politics. He was elected senator from Pennsylvania in 1857 and was a contender for the Republican 1860 presidential nomination before giving his support to Abraham Lincoln. *Courtesy Library of Congress.*

to our great joy a letter from my son Charles from Fort Union N.M. 31 May…we had not heard from him since the early part of last February."

Charles Rawn served almost his entire career as a member of the 7th Regiment of Infantry, until his promotion to major of the 24th Infantry in 1884. The 7th Infantry has a complicated history; it was organized by an act of Congress on July 16, 1798; disbanded in 1800; and revived in 1808. However in May 1815, the 7th Infantry was consolidated with the 3rd and 44th Infantry Regiments to form the 1st Infantry Regiment while the 8th, 24th and 39th were organized into a new version of the 7th Infantry. The "Cottonbalers," a nickname gained from using cotton bales to defend their positions from the British at the Battle of New Orleans, had and continues to have a proud tradition. Unfortunately, at the commencement of the Civil War, they were under the command of Major Isaac Lynde and were located in New Mexico, guarding settlers and miners from the local Indian tribes, mostly Navajos and Apaches. An aged West Pointer who graduated near the bottom of his class in 1827 and served an undistinguished thirty-four years before the war, Major Lynde was incompetent, cowardly and inefficient. He was quickly outmaneuvered and outsmarted by the Confederate forces under Lieutenant Colonel John Baylor, and seven of the ten companies of the 7th Infantry surrendered and were paroled; the other three companies were fortunately on their way from Arizona to New Mexico and were thus spared the ignominy of capture. The remnants of the 7th Infantry fought well at Valverde, New Mexico, under Colonel E.R.S. Canby in February 1862. Although a victory for Confederate brigadier general Henry Sibley, the battle turned the tide against the Confederacy in the West. While the three companies in New Mexico stayed and entered upon a campaign of maneuver and skirmish, in September 1862, the paroled men were officially exchanged and attached to the Army of the Potomac after the Battle of Antietam. Those units of the 7th Infantry fought bravely at Snicker's Gap, Fredericksburg, Chancellorsville and Gettysburg, where the decimation they suffered finished them as an effective fighting force. When the New York City draft riots broke out in 1863, what was left of the 7th Infantry was assigned to the clean-up and spent the next two years manning the harbor forts of the city, Forts Lafayette, Schuyler and Hamilton.

Second Lieutenant Charles Rawn served without distinction and saw very little action throughout the war. He was stationed for most of 1861 and early 1862 on recruitment duty at Fort Columbus and Fort Jay in New York and traveled through Fort Riley, Kansas, on his way to various forts in New Mexico (Fort Union, Fort Station, Fort Sumner and Fort Bascom) before returning to New York in May 1864. He remained at New York's Fort Schuyler, which at one time held five hundred prisoners and included a two-thousand-bed hospital; Rawn was listed as on recruitment duty there until the end of the war in April 1865. We can only imagine that his service during the Civil War was routine, administrative and dull, with perhaps the occasional skirmish on the New Mexican frontier to break the monotony. However, if routine, administrative and dull, apparently Rawn did a very good job since he was promoted to first lieutenant on July 9, 1862, and to captain on November 2, 1864.[3] He was obviously doing something right, and he continued to enjoy his father's connections in Pennsylvania.

The end of the Civil War brought enormous changes to the nation and equally enormous changes to the army's responsibilities as the southern states' futures were decided in Congress. The Reconstruction era (1865–77) meant the complete transformation of the South as directed by the Radical Republican–controlled Congress, under the leadership of Pennsylvania representative Thaddeus Stevens and Massachusetts senator Charles Sumner. This Radical Reconstruction triumphed over President Johnson's moderate position and was supported by President Grant's beliefs when he assumed the presidency in 1869. While the Radical Republicans tried to force some form of racial equality on the population, the southern whites vehemently opposed such a transition. To make Reconstruction work, the US Army became an occupying police force. As an unwelcome occupation force in a conquered territory, the army was not only despised by the southern whites, but it also faced anger and mistrust from the freed blacks. These newly freed blacks felt that the northern army, which had fought a

A modern, aerial view of historic Fort Union, New Mexico; established in 1851 to protect the Santa Fe Trail, it was abandoned in 1891. *Courtesy Library of Congress.*

war to end slavery, should side with them against their former masters, yet they soon found that the racism of the northern white soldiers was not that much different from the southern whites.

As part of the Third Military District, covering Georgia, Alabama and Florida under Generals John Pope and George Meade, Captain Rawn and the $7^{th}$ Infantry were placed into this unmanageable situation when they were transferred to Florida at the conclusion of the war. For almost four years, from May 1865 to March 1869, Rawn was assigned principally to Fort Clinch, with occasional assignments in St. Augustine and Tallahassee.

A modern aerial view of Old Fort Schuyler, New York. Fort Schuyler was built in 1833 to guard the eastern entrance to New York Harbor and was abandoned in 1911. *Courtesy SUNY Maritime College, Stephen B. Luce Library*.

The United States assumed control of what became Fort Clinch (originally established by the Spanish in 1736) with the transfer of Florida in 1822, after which the fort served as part of the country's system of coastal defense. It was seized by the Confederate forces without opposition in early 1861 as the Federal workers had already fled, and it served as a haven for Confederate blockade runners during the war. It was abandoned by the Confederates in March 1862, when General Robert E. Lee needed the troops elsewhere. Fort Clinch is located on the northernmost peninsula of Amelia Island, one of the southernmost of the Sea Islands, at the border with Georgia. Both Fernandina Beach and Amelia City are located on the island, and Jacksonville is only twenty-three miles to the southwest.

Occupied territory from 1865, Florida was formally readmitted to the Union in June 1868 and began its period of political "reconstruction" under the now-dominant congressional Radical Republicans' policy of enacting and enforcing sweeping political and racial changes. As the despised instrument of this policy, the 7$^{th}$ Infantry was hated by the southern whites and mistrusted by the freed blacks, which made for a very ugly situation. In February 1869, it finally erupted in violence.

*Left*: Radical Republican leader of the House of Representatives Thaddeus Stevens of Pennsylvania (1792–1868), 1860. *Courtesy Library of Congress.*

*Right*: Radical Republican leader of the Senate Charles Sumner of Massachusetts (1811–1874), 1860. *Courtesy Library of Congress.*

Many of the local black men and white soldiers of Fort Clinch patronized the same brothel located near the fort. With the natural addition of the overindulgence in alcohol on both sides, trouble was inevitable. Minor confrontations led to more intense confrontations between individuals and groups of antagonists until, before long, groups of blacks began hiding in ambush for the soldiers outside the brothel and beating them up, severely in some instances. In reaction to these alarming attacks on their men, the officers of the 7th Infantry began to send out patrols to find the attackers.

Regimental commander Colonel John Sprague reported the explosion that happened on February 22, when a patrol was attacked:

> [A] *patrol…was fired upon by a band of armed negroes, secreted in the bushes, without a warning. One of the patrol was mortally wounded and died the next day. The soldiers under Captain* [Charles] *Rawn… assembled and pursued the negroes, and followed them into the city, where an indiscriminate firing took place, both by negroes and soldiers, when one*

Fort Clinch, Florida, was built in 1847 after the Second Seminole War on the remains of a 1736 Spanish fortification. It was abandoned after the Spanish-American War. *Courtesy Library of Congress.*

> *colored man was killed. The affair has been greatly exaggerated...arising from political prejudice, and the natural antipathy here to the vigilant exertion of the military.*[4]

In the aftermath of Rawn's actions, a riot almost erupted as tempers on both sides flared. Leaders of the black community demanded that Captain Rawn be held responsible and were disgusted when he was only fined for breaking the peace. Not surprisingly, the area's white population volunteered to pay his entire fine. Throughout this time, Rawn's superior, Colonel Sprague, defended his captain. Sprague contended that it was known that a group of one hundred or more blacks had been planning to attack the fort and that Rawn's actions had saved the camp from a possible disastrous attack that would have seen a lot more bloodshed. This statement is probably an example of a superior officer protecting his subordinate, but one can imagine Captain Rawn and his men thrown into a situation where they had to react to a real threat, and it is amazing that other such confrontations or worse did not occur. As Colonel Sprague also wrote: "The military in this quarter are surrounded by enemies, and unless encouraged, even sustained, their exertions will be futile. Cattle and hogs are shot down at the white man's door, and the colored man, as well as the lawless white assassins, or robbers, roams at large, gun in hand, in utter defiance of any authority."[5]

But Florida was not only a firestorm of racial tension; it was a most inhospitable area for other reasons as well. Sickness among the troops was pervasive due to exposure, overexertion, poor nourishment and the prevalence of insects and germs. Men suffered from many different diseases, with dysentery and malaria being the most common. Charles Rawn succumbed to the latter at some point during his Reconstruction duty in Florida, along with many of his fellow soldiers. Caused by a mosquito bite from an adult female mosquito, the symptoms of malaria include chills, shakes, nausea, headaches, an enlarged spleen and fever. During and after the Civil War, malaria was not often fatal because of the ready availability of quinine, but it killed roughly thirty thousand soldiers during the war, while around three million contracted the disease. Already suffering from periods of ill health, Rawn would suffer from malarial symptoms throughout the rest of his life, and it would be a major contributing cause of his death.

One can only imagine the joy and relief that the men of the 7$^{th}$ Infantry felt when they received their orders to leave Florida for the frontier. Ironically, they would be entering another area of tremendous racial tension compounded by irreconcilable cultural differences. It would not be an easy transition.

CHAPTER 3

# THE FRONTIER ARMY

The army that Captain Rawn was now serving in on the frontier was a very different army than the one that had won the Civil War. In the aftermath of that war, the regular army became a small force, reduced in size by Congress, maintained as an unnecessary drain on the taxpayer and scorned by the public that had just suffered through four horrific years of carnage. By 1866, the army had dwindled from 1 million to a mere 30,000 soldiers—not nearly enough to meet the demands of the thousands of settlers, farmers, ranchers, miners, businessmen and others who were now streaming to the West by wagon train, stagecoach, steamboat and railroad. In July 1866, Congress increased the army to 54,000, with forty-five infantry regiments, ten cavalry regiments and five artillery regiments. Enlistments were set at three years for the infantry and five years for the cavalry. Each infantry regiment consisted of ten companies, each cavalry regiment of twelve companies ("troops") and each artillery regiment of twelve companies ("batteries"). While each cavalry regiment was commanded by a colonel, with one lieutenant colonel in support, the smaller infantry regiment was commanded by a major, with companies commanded by a captain, assisted by a first and second lieutenant. The fixed strength of a company was set at 64 privates, raised to 100 in 1867, raising the total number of soldiers to 56,815 on paper. Unfortunately, most companies existed at half strength.[6]

The War Department was made up of ten administrative and technical bureaus. The Adjutant General's Department was in charge of orders and commands and was the custodian of the army's records, while the Inspector

General's Department inspected and reported on the proficiency, discipline and leadership within the army. The Judge Advocate General's Department reviewed the authority of the military courts; the Quartermaster's Department provided quarters and many of the supplies; the Subsistence Department supplied the men's rations; health and hygiene were overseen by the Medical Department; the Pay Department distributed wages; mapping and construction were under the purview of the Corps of Engineers; arms and ammunition were provided by the Ordnance Department; and the Signal Corps was responsible for communication, primarily through the use of flags, torches and the telegraph.[7]

Meanwhile, the officer corps had to be restructured. Regular officers who had achieved high rank in volunteer regiments during the war reverted to their regular grade or tried to obtain a higher grade in new regiments; in this way, a general became a colonel, major or even captain, while former colonels and majors became lieutenants. Brevet promotions, giving an officer a higher rank for gallantry but without the authority, precedence or pay of a real promotion in rank, had been easy to obtain during wartime services. But they were not just empty honors since officers were assigned to commands according to that rank.[8] In 1870, to make the system less confusing and function better, Congress decreed that brevet officers had to wear the uniform of their regular rank and were to be addressed by that rank.[9] That Captain Rawn had not obtained a brevet rank further indicates his lack of actual combat experience, but the fact that he maintained his rank as captain demonstrates the value in which the army held his service.

The army was divided into two divisions in the West, roughly along the Continental Divide: the Division of the Missouri, under Lieutenant General William Sherman, was headquartered in St. Louis; Major General Henry Halleck commanded the Division of the Pacific from San Francisco. The Division of the Missouri was divided into the Department of the Missouri under Major General Winfield Scott Hancock, who was responsible for Missouri, Kansas, Colorado and New Mexico; the Department of the Platte under Brevet Major General Philip St. George Cooke, who covered Iowa, Nebraska, Utah and portions of the Dakotas and Montana; and the Department of Dakota, including Minnesota and the other parts of the Dakotas and Montana, which was under the command of Major General Alfred Terry. In the Pacific, California, Nevada and Arizona were in the Department of California under Brevet Major General Irvin McDowell, and Oregon, Washington and Idaho were in the Department of the Columbia under Brevet Major General Frederick Steele.[10]

When General Grant became president in 1869, Sherman was promoted to a four-star general. As a soldier, he hated the political atmosphere of Washington, but he managed to stamp the frontier army with his fierce personality. At the same time, he was forced to preside over the reduction of the army to 37,313 in 1869 and 27,000 in 1874. These reductions were accomplished by attrition in the enlisted ranks, while 900 surplus officers were eliminated through resignation and retirement, sometimes forced.[11] Rawn survived all the cuts. The plethora of officers and the rigidity of the seniority system stagnated promotions for three decades; it would be over twenty years before Rawn was promoted to major. Meanwhile, the real measure of all these cuts was felt most at the company level. While the number of units stayed the same, the number of soldiers decreased drastically until the typical infantry company numbered 41, including 29 privates, in 1881. Given men who were sick, wounded, deserted, imprisoned, detached and detailed to daily and extra duty, companies were lucky to muster 25 men. With 430 companies to man 200 western posts, the company became the army's basic tactical unit, not the regiment.

Pay scales were fixed in 1870, with rates from $3,500 per year for a colonel to $1,400 for a second lieutenant. With the cost of his own uniform, frequent changes in station and the high cost of goods and services on the frontier, that pay did not go far. The enlisted men fared no better, although they did have a clothing allowance; a private made $13 per month, while a line sergeant made $22. The paymaster arrived irregularly and came with currency that had to be converted to coin at a discount of 12 to 40 percent. Automatically deducted from the men's pay were their fees to the post laundresses and any charges made at the post traders. Any remaining funds quickly went to pay off other debts they had accumulated since their last pay and for gambling, alcohol, female companionship, etc. It

General William T. Sherman (1829–1891), 1865. *Courtesy Library of Congress.*

was never long until they were in debt again. As frontier Corporal E.A. Bode remembered:

> *Payday was always a holiday and duly celebrated by all concerned. Buying necessary articles, spending foolishly, or on whiskey and gambling, the money was generally invested and nothing left for most,* [other] *than the hope of another payday. If one or more were unlucky enough to have their pay taken by a court-martial there was always a dollar or so left to gamble with, trusting their luck for drinks.*[12]

Besides receiving poor pay, soldiers were looked down on with condescension and contempt, suffered under horrible living conditions and were subject to harsh discipline. Recruits were typically men of lower-than-average intelligence, physical fitness and motivation. The army drew heavily on the urban poor, and it is estimated that between 1865 and 1874, half of the recruits were born in a foreign country, with 20 percent coming from Ireland. Many of the immigrants did not speak English, yet many of them had served in the militaries in their home countries, adapted quickly and advanced to noncommissioned officers' ranks. With so little to commend itself to staying in the army, it is not surprising that in 1871, after a reduction in pay in 1870, the desertion rate was 32.6 percent. Given the horrible living conditions, low pay, low morale, desertion and severe discipline, turnover was rapid. This, plus the near total absence of formal training, with only rudimentary instruction provided at the recruitment depots in Missouri, New York and Ohio, meant that the frontier army was an inexperienced and poorly prepared one.[13] The only support they had was themselves, and men felt a loyalty to their companies because they usually served their entire enlistment in the same company; lived, fought and drilled together; and served under the same officers, usually at the same fort.

Not only did the frontier army suffer from inadequate manpower and resources, but it was also unclear where the division of authority and responsibility lay in regard to Indian policy with respect to the Bureau of Indian Affairs within the Department of the Interior. With conflicting aims and missions between the bureau and the army, it was difficult to understand, let alone implement, any comprehensive policy. Ultimately, three conditions defined the army's new mission: the army was set against an enemy where friends and enemies could not be clearly identified, frontier service placed the army in opposition to people who aroused conflicting emotions and the foe was unconventional in techniques and in the aim of warfare. In effect, the army had to become one large police force, and with a small force, strategy on the ground dictated that the army combine dispersion for defense with temporary concentration for offense, while the broader strategy was to systematically pacify and settle the frontier by advancing a steady line of forts.[14]

To equip the frontier army was a major consideration given the far-flung system of forts. Soldiers were clothed in surplus Civil War uniforms stored in warehouses that were infested with mold, mildew and insects, and the uniforms were of single weight, hot in summer and cold in winter. There were numerous defects in cut, sizing and quality, largely due to profiteering and corruption, and most of the surplus sizes were too small or too large. The standard uniform coat was a snug-fitting, dark-blue, woolen, single-breasted frock with a long skirt adopted in 1857. The trousers were light blue, trimmed in the color of the arm of service. The high-crowned Kossuth hat, with a turned-up brim on one side and decorated with ostrich feathers, was impractical, cumbersome and fragile, although very stylish. The 1872 campaign hat was black with an unusually wide brim that could be hooked on to the crown, but it soon lost its sizing and tended to fall apart in the rain. The 1876 hat was more orthodox, with a smaller brim, but was not much better for comfort or durability. The kepi, or forage cap, was more functional but still offered little protection and was hard to keep on. The result was a plethora of all kinds of hats as men and officers adapted issued hats or purchased their own. While the enlisted made do with uniforms supplied by the Quartermaster's Department, the officers purchased their own, better-quality uniforms from private vendors approved by the Quartermaster's Department. New uniforms were proposed in 1872, but the quartermaster general's report of 1873 listed large surpluses of older uniforms being sold at auction, and the penurious Congress halted the development of the new uniforms, despite the fact that the old uniforms were all outdated, unfit and of the wrong sizes. Change came gradually, and it would not be until the late 1870s that official winter uniforms were created with arctic overcoats, caps, gauntlets and boots made out of buffalo, beaver, seal, muskrat and sheepskin. The 1870s witnessed a more professional approach to design and manufacturing, and a foundation was eventually laid of documented specifications for clothing and equipment, while the Industrial Revolution brought improved technology and manufacturing methods. By 1880, the trend was finally toward a more practical field outfit.[15]

While improvements in clothing came slowly, the most significant advances came about in weapons technology. The breech-loading rifle with metallic

Staff officers, line officers and enlisted men uniforms, 1850–61, H.A. Ogden print. *Courtesy Library of Congress.*

cartridges was first developed and used on a limited basis during the Civil War, but by the end of the war, all of the regular army was equipped with the modified Springfield. In 1872, the arms board convened under General Terry and approved the 1873 Springfield rifle and carbine, which were used, with periodic improvements, for the next twenty years. The early 1870s also saw the metallic-cartridge pistol replace the cap-and-ball six-shooter. The .45-caliber Colt 1872 revolver was the favorite of the army and was known as

Officers, enlisted men, cavalry and artillery uniforms, 1872–81, H.A. Ogden print. *Courtesy Library of Congress.*

"the Peacemaker," although other models were produced by Remington and Smith and Wesson. Bayonets were of two kinds: a long, narrow, detachable blade that locked onto the front of the rifle was simply a weapon; the shorter and wider bayonet with a pointed end, the Rice (or trowel) bayonet, was used as a weapon and an entrenching tool. The first was good for hand-to-hand combat situations in the Civil War but not on the frontier, and the second did not work well as either a weapon or a tool and was obsolete by

Guard mount in buffalo coats at Fort Keogh, Montana, photograph by L.A. Huffman, 1879. *Courtesy the Montana Historical Society Research Center, Montana Historical Society, Helena, Montana.*

the late 1870s, although it did help save the lives of many soldiers of the 7th Infantry at the Battle of the Big Hole in 1877.

While the Indians were surprised by the improved weapons, they soon were in possession of them and excelled in their use. But the army also had two new weapons that the Indians could not adapt to: the Hotchkiss mountain howitzer and the Gatling gun. The twelve-pounder mountain howitzer was most popular and effective, capable of firing rapidly up to four thousand yards. The Gatling gun had multiple barrels that were turned by a crank and fed bullets from a hopper. It was capable of firing up to 350 rounds per minute, but it was generally regarded as useless since it was short range, easily fouled with the refuse of the black powder cartridges and jammed when overheated.[16]

By 1871, the 7th Infantry was scattered among the various forts in Montana, with regimental headquarters at Fort Shaw. Located along the Sun River, twenty-five miles above the junction of the Missouri River and positioned on the Mullan Military Road, it was established to guard the traffic between Fort Benton, the head of navigation for the Missouri River, and the gold rush town of Helena. Captain Rawn did not immediately

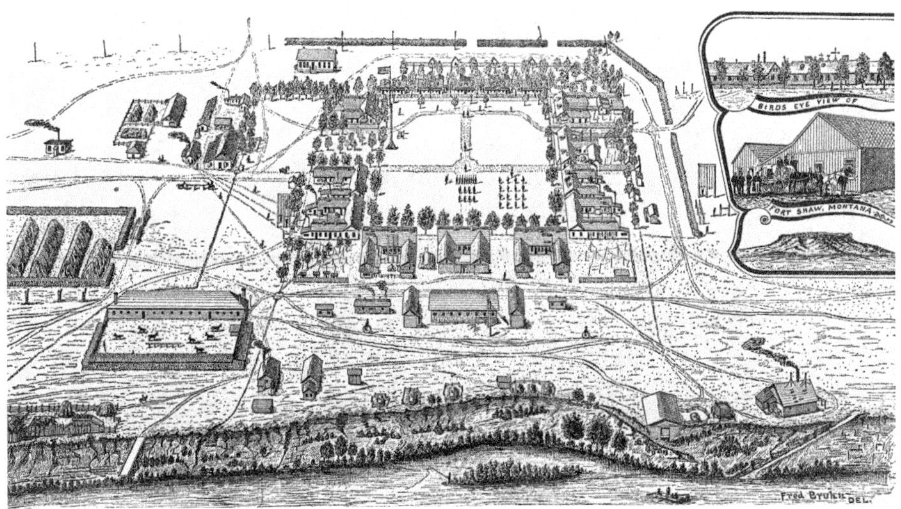


Letterhead showing Fort Shaw, Montana, from a letter in the T.C. Power Collection, addressed to J.H. McKnight & Co., no date. *Courtesy the Montana Historical Society Research Center, Montana Historical Society, Helena, Montana.*

Fort Buford, Dakota Territory. Watercolor of the new 1871 fort just after it was rebuilt. The barracks are on the right and officers' quarters on the left, with the parade ground in the center. *Courtesy the State Historical Society of North Dakota.*

proceed to Montana and was reported on detached duty first at Fort Snelling, Minnesota, and then at Fort Fred Steele, Wyoming, until mid-1870. He was then stationed at Fort Buford in the Dakota Territory through May 1872, when he joined the rest of the 7th Infantry at Fort Shaw. He remained in Montana until mid-1879 and was frequently left in command during Colonel John Gibbon's absences.[17]

Typically, fort life in the 1870s was largely boring. A typical day started with reveille at 6:00 a.m., followed by inspection and first roll call at 6:15 a.m., morning stable call at 6:30 a.m., mess call at 7:00 a.m., fatigue duty at 7:30 a.m. and an 8:00 a.m. sick call. Then came assembly of the guard and guard mount at 8:30 a.m., drill at 10:00 a.m., mess call at noon, drill or target practice (usually one or two shots per man per month) at 1:00 p.m., fatigue duty at 2:00 p.m., stable call at 4:00 p.m., assembly and dress parade fifteen minutes before sunset, retreat and second roll call at sunset, 9:00 p.m. tattoo and third roll call and, finally, taps and lights out at 9:30 p.m.[18] Guard duty was the most important duty; assigned by rotation, the soldiers on guard duty remained in uniform with equipment ready for an entire twenty-four-hour duty shift. These pickets, or sentries, changed every two hours and followed very specific protocols on challenging, saluting and reporting. Fatigue duty was the name for any work detail that consisted of nonmilitary tasks involving manual labor; these jobs were usually hard and monotonous, and the men were under close supervision by officers. Special duties might include serving as cook, office servant, hospital orderly, scout or clerk. Patrols and escort duty broke the tedium and provided a sense of excitement as they escorted civilian wagon trains, the paymaster or others.[19] All behavior was strictly monitored.

Anyone caught breaking the rules was subject to various levels of discipline. For minor violations, extra duties might be assigned or one might be confined to quarters. Other punishments included a fine, flogging, hanging by the thumbs, carrying a log or cannonball around the post or, more conventionally, a term in the guardhouse. More serious crimes merited a court-martial that could result in long-term punishments, reduction in rank, dishonorable discharge or death, depending on the infraction.[20]

Food was a major concern to all soldiers. The rations provided by the army tended to be plentiful and palatable enough for survival and were usually supplemented with produce grown on post gardens and game shot in the area. Food in the field would depend on the supply trains but could never be considered pleasant, as it consisted primarily of salted meat, hardtack, coffee and sugar, perhaps with some dried fruit or beans. Prior to 1872, cooking in the field was done by the company; after that time, personal cooking gear was provided to each soldier to cook his own meal. The mess kit consisted of a frying pan with a shallow tin plate as a lid; other utensils included a tin cup, knife, fork and spoon. The meat was generally boiled and then fried. Hardtack was typically immersed in liquid to soften it enough to be edible. Coffee, heavily sweetened with sugar, was the most indispensable part of any meal and one of the few pleasures available to the soldiers, warming them up in cold, wet weather and keeping them awake in the face of danger.[21]

Half of a soldier's time would be spent on post duty and the other half would be in the field, with actual combat time being very infrequent. However, danger was never too far away. While there were few frontal assaults on forts, the Indians excelled at sudden raids on small details or individuals who left the fort unescorted. Despite these dangers, while on the post, the men had many hours to kill in the evenings and at other times. For amusement, soldiers gambled on cards, dice or whatever they could; they also entertained themselves with storytelling, dancing, singing and reading. Fraternal organizations were also popular. While at Fort Buford, Dakota Territory, Rawn was a charter officer of Masonic Yellowstone Lodge #88, which included General Asa Blunt as the worshipful master and Captain Richard Comba, Lieutenant William Logan and Lieutenant William English. When the 7th Infantry transferred to Fort Shaw, the lodge lost almost all of its members and had to surrender its charter.[22]

Since there were few opportunities for sex, men had little choice but to use the prostitutes in the area. These prostitutes were not allowed on the post, but some took jobs as laundresses to get access, and some laundresses turned to prostitution to make more money. But generally the men went to town or to a nearby "hog ranch," which also provided gambling and drinking options.[23] Drinking was by far the favorite method of entertainment and self-medication. In the 1880s, no less than 4 percent of the soldiers were hospitalized as alcoholics, at a time when "alcoholism" meant suffering with advanced delirium tremens or some equally grave condition.[24]

Supporting the fort's infrastructure were the army sutlers and post traders. The post sutler existed from 1821 to 1860 and was a civilian merchant licensed to sell provisions to the army to make up for the deficiencies in the army supply network. The successful sutler was an integral part of the army with a rank, a home and a sense of permanence. However, the demands of the Civil War and the abuse of the system resulted in Congress eliminating the position in preference of the army supplying its own needs. This quickly proved unworkable, and in 1870, the secretary of war authorized one or

The old post trader's store at Fort Buford, Dakota Territory, used from 1856 until 1872. With its log walls and dirt roof, it is typical of the early military posts along the Upper Missouri River. *Courtesy the Montana Historical Society Research Center, Montana Historical Society, Helena, Montana.*

more trading establishments to be maintained at any military post on the frontier not in the vicinity of a town or city. While the sutler had been a specialized profession, the post trader was more generic, and his primary license and general behavior were controlled by army approval, usually by a post council of administration that established rates and prices and determined the rate of profit. It was natural that the post trader fended for himself and extended his operations and often became a center of social interaction for the entire area.[25]

When the 7th Infantry arrived at Fort Shaw in 1870, some quarters were still unfinished; all four company quarters lacked shingles, only two buildings were protected by outside plaster, the storehouses were inadequate and the stable and corrals needed work.[26] Fortunately for the 7th Infantry, Fort Shaw became a comparative oasis. A vegetable garden was tried, succeeded, expanded and irrigated. Wild game was easily available, and the post soon had a bakery. Still, men had to occasionally dip into their pay to supplement their rations. As a luxury, a sewer system of tile pipe drained the compound, helping to keep a clean and healthy environment. Colonel Gibbon established a library, and the regimental band stationed at the fort performed for many functions. The officers, wives and soldiers formed a repertoire company, and a playhouse was built, 125 feet long, 35 feet wide and 24 feet deep, with dressing rooms and property rooms in an ell addition.[27] Frances Marie Antoinette Mack Roe, who accompanied her officer husband around the frontier, described a performance at Fort Shaw in January 1879:

> *Our little entertainment for the benefit of the mission here was a wonderful success. Every seat was occupied, every corner packed, and we were afraid that the old theater might collapse. We made eighty dollars, clear of all expenses. The tableaux were first, so the small people could be sent home early. Then came our pantomime. Sergeant Thompson sang the words and the orchestra played a soft accompaniment that made the whole thing most effective. Major Pierce was a splendid Villikins, and as Dinah I received enough applause to satisfy anyone, but the curtain remained down, motionless and unresponsive, just because I happened to be the wife of the stage manager!*[28]

It was not long after Rawn's arrival at Fort Shaw that his history of ill health continued. On January 15, 1873, Rawn suffered a "complete dislocation backward of the right foot complicated with incomplete flexion

View of officers' row, Fort Shaw, Montana, in 1889, when it was the station of four companies of the 25th Infantry. *Courtesy the National Archives, copy provided by the Montana Historical Society Research Center, Montana Historical Society, Helena, Montana.*

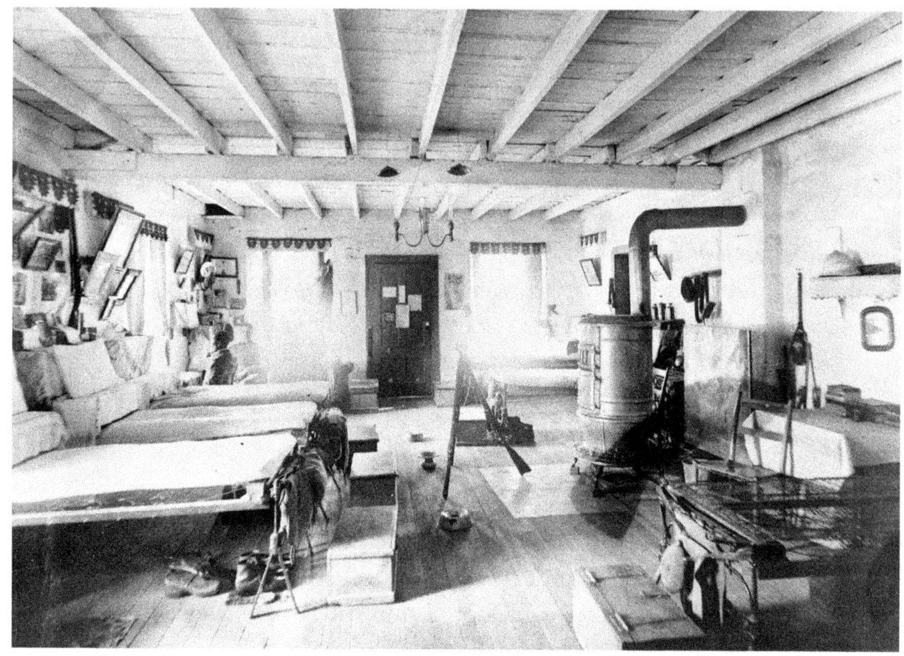

Interior view of the enlisted men's barracks at Fort Shaw, 1888–1901. *Courtesy the Montana Historical Society Research Center, Montana Historical Society, Helena, Montana.*

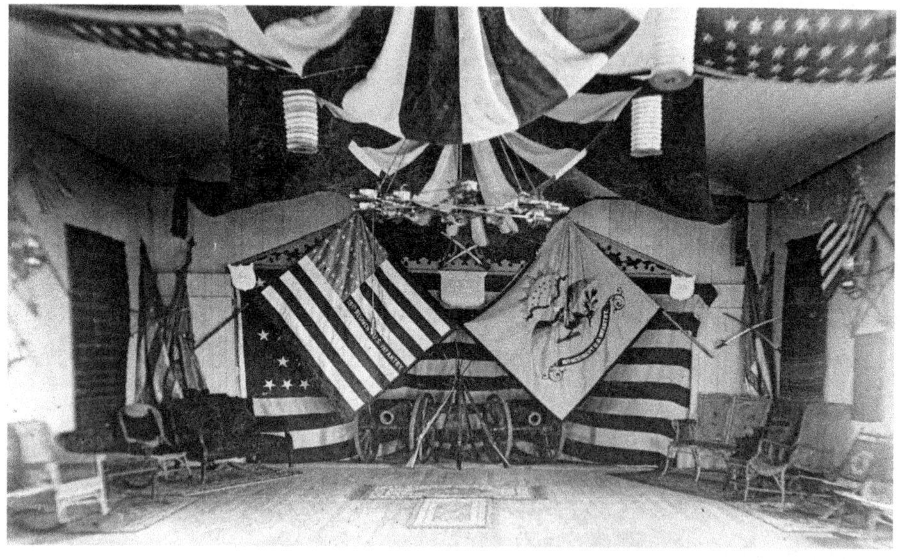

Decorations for a ball for the 15th Infantry at Fort Buford, Dakota Territory, 1882. *Courtesy the State Historical Society of North Dakota.*

and extension of the right foot complicated with lateral motion, pain with tendency to renewal of inflammation under long continued use (or walking over rough) or frozen ground."[29] Besides dislocating his foot, he also fractured his tibia. The nature and date of the injury suggests that he fell from his horse on icy ground and his foot was caught in the stirrup while he was dragged for some distance. He remained confined to quarters until May 23 and then took sick leave in Harrisburg until April 28, 1874. While on leave, on March 26, he married twenty-three-year-old Isabel Douglas Nauman at an Episcopal church in Lancaster, thirty miles from Harrisburg. Isabel was the daughter of Mary Dummett and Colonel George Nauman (1802–1863), who was a graduate of West Point and served in the artillery in the Florida and Mexican Wars, where he was commended for meritorious service and received a brevet commission. He became chief of artillery at Newport News, Virginia, during the Civil War before his death from sunstroke.[30] Like many officers' wives, Isabel accompanied her husband to his various posts, probably traveling by steamboat to Fort Benton and then by wagon to Fort Shaw, a distance of about sixty miles.[31]

Officer and family in front of Fort Shaw officers' quarters in 1889. *Courtesy the National Archives, copy provided by the Montana Historical Society Research Center, Montana Historical Society, Helena, Montana.*

An army wife's life was never easy. Typically from a middle-class Victorian home in the East, the officer's wife had to face the demands of a lonely, harsh and dangerous existence. A wife's job was to care for her husband, provide him with a home and hearth and supportive environment, bear him children and provide those children with the proper moral and religious upbringing. Yet this was an alien world of people and customs where the innocent eastern woman found herself exposed to gambling, drinking, prostitution, Indians, danger and excitement. The reality of life in the West quickly overwhelmed accustomed norms, and these women would never be the same. A wife frequently became the de facto head of the house in her husband's frequent absences and would do her best through talent, perseverance and ingenuity to succeed; in some instances, the commanding officer's wife even became de facto commander of the fort.

Living conditions were often horrendous. Wives were forced at times to live in tents, with substandard accommodations and furniture made of crates or barrels; the food was often suspect and sometimes in short supply; and shifts in weather brought sudden and violent changes. They had to deal with animals, snakes and drunken soldiers; occasionally, they even found half-naked Indians wandering around in their living quarters. These challenges led women to discover that they had the courage and ability to adapt and succeed. Forced to interact with other wives, laundresses, prostitutes, Indians, Chinese and female servants, they were also forced to revise the nature of discrimination.[32] Maria Hunter, wife of Major David Hunter, wrote that a perfect army wife "never annoys…[her husband] with trifles, adapts herself perfectly to every situation, never frets at inconvenience, makes him perfectly comfortable, entertains company handsomely, and makes a delightful life for him."[33] But the reality of being an officer's wife took a resilience and adaptability not required in the East, and it changed them.

The army provided an officer with accommodations for himself and two horses, fuel and light for his quarters and food for his horse. Everything else, including moving expenses for his family, had to come from his meager pay. Weight allowance for a lieutenant's personal baggage—furniture, housewares, clothes, books, etc. for his entire family—was one thousand pounds; everything else had to be shipped by civilian freight haulers at two dollars per pound in 1878. Once on post, the army wife found that servants, so common in the East, were hard to obtain and harder to keep. Young female servants were preferred but often were married within a short time; enlisted men assigned to duty, "strikers," were the second choice, and success depended on their quality, personality, control and loyalty. (Congress outlawed using strikers in 1870, but the law was frequently ignored.) Other potential servants were Chinese, Mexican and Indian depending on the post's location.[34]

One totally new experience for the army wife was the practice of being "ranked out." A superior officer arriving at a post could evict any subordinate officer from his quarters and make them his own. Frances Roe unhappily wrote from Fort Shaw in 1882:

> *YOU will be shocked, I know, when you hear that we are houseless—homeless—that for a second time Faye has been ranked out of quarters! At Camp Supply the turn out was swift, but this time it has been long drawn out and most vexatious. Last month Major Bagley came here from Fort Maginnis, and as we had rather expected that he would select our house, we made no preparations for winter previous to his coming. But as soon as he reached the post, and many times after, he assured Faye that nothing could possibly induce him to disturb us, and said many more sweet things.*
>
> *Unfortunately for us, he was ordered to return to Fort Maginnis to straighten out some of his accounts while quartermaster, and Mrs. Bagley decided to remain as she was until Major Bagley's return...Having faith in Major Bagley's word, the house was cleaned from top to bottom, much painting and calcimining having been done. All the floors were painted and hard-oiled, and everyone knows what discomfort that always brings about. But at last everything was finished, and we were about to settle down to the enjoyment of a tidy, cheerful little home when Major Bagley appeared the second time, and within two hours Faye was notified that his quarters had been selected by him!*[35]

Besides housing, a major concern, not only for the army wife but for everyone, was the poor quality of health on the frontier. While the West was advertised as healthy and invigorating, with clean, crisp, fresh air and wide-open spaces, the reality was far different. Marginal diet, substandard quarters, lack of adequate medical care, danger from men and animals and a limited number of doctors made staying healthy difficult. Nearly everyone suffered at one point from cholera, typhoid fever, malarial fever, diarrhea, dysentery, tuberculosis, tonsillitis, epidemic catarrh (upper respiratory infection), venereal disease, rheumatism or phthisis (consumption). Nor was there any psychiatric care available to combat the effects of isolation, boredom and danger, which led to the abuse of alcohol as an escape. Medical care typically consisted of prescribed doses of morphine, cocaine, heroin and opium available over the counter. Home remedies and snake oil remedies frequently relied on alcohol as a base. Sometimes it worked.

But there was no cure for one of the greatest killers of the era: childbirth. Motherhood was considered the fulfilment of a woman's destiny; some medical books recommended having a child every twenty months. Childbirth back east was difficult enough, but with the harsher conditions of the frontier, it was much worse. Babies were often delivered premature due to rough traveling, and scarcely any time was allowed for recuperation before the travel recommenced. Doctors were often unavailable. It is not surprising that many women tried to avoid pregnancy. In the 1870s, contraception through the use of rubber condoms and the rhythm method were developed, but books describing them were considered obscene and the authors went to jail. Once pregnant, there was only one solution: abortion. In the East, there were advertisements for female monthly pills or French periodic pills, while powerful abortifacients like cottonroot, snakeroot and savin were available for ten dollars. However, on the frontier, women had to improvise and used post-coital douches made with vinegar or baking soda or inserted goose quills to induce abortion.[36]

But children were expected, and Charles and Isabel were typical frontier parents, producing four children. The first two were born in Montana Territory: Charles in February 1875 at Fort Shaw; Margaret in August 1877

Schoolchildren in front of the post school at Fort Keogh, Montana, 1891. *Courtesy the Montana Historical Society Research Center, Montana Historical Society, Helena, Montana.*

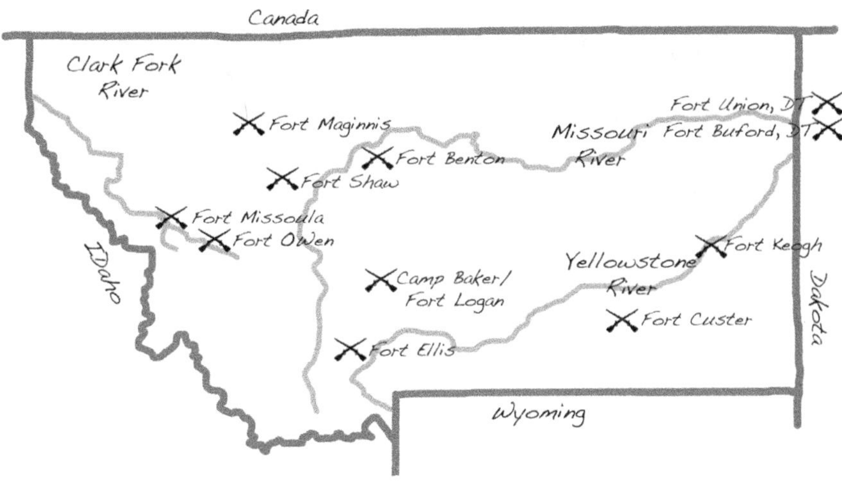


Map of the principal frontier forts in Montana. *Courtesy Bryan Steward, artist, 2015.*

at Fort Missoula; Douglas at Fort Stevenson, Dakota Territory, in February 1882; and Isabel at Fort Elliott, Texas, in October 1885. For many children, the time spent on the frontier was remembered as one of adventure and amusement, with the family's striker a glorified playmate. Boys were less circumscribed than girls, but all enjoyed riding, picnics, croquet, tennis, baseball, shooting, sleighing, swimming and holidays. Post schools were authorized in 1866, but it was not until the 1881 army reorganization that guidelines were established for all post commanders to follow. Soldiers who acted as teachers received thirty-five cents per day extra-duty pay, and if the teacher had no authority to mete out corporal punishment, a call to the post adjutant or a note to the parents quickly solved the problem. But due to the migratory nature of service on the frontier, education inevitably suffered.[37]

Life in the frontier army, in short, was not easy.

Meanwhile, opposing the frontier army in Montana was an Indian population of over 30,000 in 1872. This included approximately 7,500 Blackfeet; 4,790 Assiniboines; 1,100 Gros Ventres; 2,625 Sioux; 4,140 Crows; 460 Salishes; 1,000 Pend d'Oreilles; 320 Kootenais; 677 Shoshones; 8,000 "roving" Sioux; and some Northern Cheyennes, Chippewas and Crees.[38]

They were not happy.

CHAPTER 4

# THE BATTLE OF PRYOR'S CREEK

Corporal E.A. Bode succinctly summarized the Indian situation in his memoirs: "As the Indians are at present [1884–89] they are at the mercy of the agent and are driven through his dishonesty on the warpath. Whites infringe on the rights of the Indians and cheat them at every turn. Some colonel of the Army, anguished to better his record, assists in a general kick and drives them on the warpath."[39] If one adds to that list the abrogation of treaty rights and the theft of Indian lands, the nature of the frontier wars of 1864 to 1890 is clearly defined.

The problem did not begin or end in Montana, but Montana would suffer greatly. The 1851 Treaty of Fort Laramie recognized a vast territory as Cheyenne and Arapaho land, an area including parts of Wyoming, Colorado and Kansas. But the discovery of gold in 1858 led to a new treaty that ceded most of that land to the United States. Some of the Indians did not accept the new treaty and continued to hunt on the earlier reservation land. War with the Indians broke out in early 1864, culminating in the Battle of Sand Creek on November 29, 1864, when Colonel John Chivington's column of seven hundred Colorado volunteers attacked and destroyed a peaceful village of Cheyennes and Arapahos. At the end of the day, some two hundred Cheyennes—mostly women and children—were dead, and the traditional power of the Cheyenne was destroyed forever.[40]

With the discovery of gold in Montana in 1862–63, miners began streaming to the area using the new Bozeman Trail through land guaranteed to the Sioux. To protect the miners coming to the gold fields, the government established Forts Reno, Phil Kearny and C.F. Smith along the trail. At Fort Laramie in June 1866, Red Cloud, of the Oglala Sioux, made a speech about the perfidy of the white man and vowed resistance. Waiting for his opportunity, Red Cloud attacked a party of eighty soldiers under Brevet Colonel William Fetterman, sent out from Fort Phil Kearny to relieve a wood train from Indian attack on December 21, 1866. When Fetterman pursued the Sioux beyond the limits of his orders, Red Cloud sprung his ambush, and all eighty-one soldiers were killed. Eventually, Red Cloud's War forced the US government to abandon the Bozeman Trail at the Fort Laramie Treaty of 1868, which also guaranteed Sioux ownership of the Black Hills, with hunting rights in South Dakota, Montana and Wyoming. Additionally, the Powder River country was closed to the whites.[41]

There were other battles: the Hayfield Fight of 1867, when the Cheyenne and Sioux attacked soldiers and civilians cutting hay near Fort C.F. Smith in Montana; the Wagon Box Fight, the day after the Hayfield Fight, when Red Cloud led a force against contractors cutting wood west of Fort Phil Kearny; Beecher's Island Battle in 1868, in eastern Colorado; the Battle of Washita River in 1868, in present-day Oklahoma; and the 1869 Battle of Summit Springs, in Colorado.[42] Things were only heating up.

The election of Ulysses Grant as president in 1868 gave hope to the military that with a former general as commander in chief, reform would favor the military and the Bureau of Indian Affairs would be returned to the War Department—beyond civilian control and corruption. However, "President" Grant was not "General" Grant and was receptive to humanitarian reform impulses. The resultant "Peace Policy" was to be a conquest of peace, with civilian supremacy. Agents and superintendents were nominated by church groups, the Board of Indian Commissioners was composed of philanthropists serving without pay and the new treaty system treated the Indian tribes as dependent domestic nations. The aim was to educate, Christianize and assimilate—not annihilate. The army was to maintain responsibility over Indians outside the reservation, but the separation of responsibility over friendly and hostile off-reservation Indians was unclear.[43] The Peace Policy was not going to work.

On June 4, 1869, Colonel Philippe Regis de Trobriand arrived at Fort Shaw to take command of the Montana Military District, while commanding at Fort Ellis, near Bozeman, was Major Eugene Baker. Baker had graduated twelfth in the West Point class of 1859 and served with distinction during the Civil War, but the boredom and stress of frontier duty led him to drinking. He took four companies of the 2nd Cavalry to Fort Shaw, where he met with

President Ulysses S. Grant (1822–1885, president 1869–77) at his cottage by the sea in 1872. *Courtesy Library of Congress.*

Colonel de Trobriand and was ordered to arrest five Indians indicted for the murder of Malcomb Clark; he was also to arrest Mountain Chief and thirteen others of the Piegan Blackfeet tribe known as troublemakers. General Philip Sheridan's recommendation was that "if the lives and property of citizens of Montana can be protected by striking Mountain Chief's band, I want them struck. Tell Baker to strike them hard."[44]

On January 23, 1870, Baker's scouts misidentified a village along the Marias River. Under the influence of alcohol, Baker ordered the troops to strike, and 173 innocent Blackfeet, including 53 women and children, were killed. Baker left Lieutenant Doane to finish the destruction of the innocent village and the capture of the 140 women and children left while he futilely went in pursuit of Mountain Chief. While Baker was congratulated by his superiors, the eastern press vilified him for the Marias (or Baker) Massacre, and public opinion convicted him of unspeakable barbarianism.[45]

The Peace Policy limped along while wars in the Southwest against the Apache and against the Modoc in California and Oregon made the situation worse; but it was access to the gold fields, development of the railroad and the Sioux War that doomed it.

Starting in 1870, the Northern Pacific Railroad advanced westward from Minnesota into the Dakota Territory to the Missouri River and eastward from the Washington Territory, until by 1872 there was only a 225-mile section left to complete between Coulson's Crossing (present-day Billings) and Glendive, Montana, along the Yellowstone River Valley. But this land had been guaranteed to the Sioux, and the Hunkpapa leader, Sitting Bull, had vowed to stop the incursion.

According to the charter for financier Jay Cooke and Company's transcontinental Northern Pacific Railroad, the government was required to provide military protection for its surveying expeditions. With Sitting Bull's threats well known, when Colonel John Gibbon, the new commander of the District of Montana at Fort Shaw, assembled the army escort for the 1872 expedition, there was every reason to believe that there would be trouble.[46] The 1872 western survey crew was led by Ferdinand Hayden, and the escort was commanded by Major Baker. An enlisted man, William White, described Baker as a "hardhearted man" and "a heavy drinker." Apparently Baker's drinking was so well known that when he died in 1884 at Fort Walla Walla, Washington, his West Point obituary stated that "like so many officers of fine physique, believing that nothing could injure his constitution, [Baker] neglected such precautions as he might have taken and broke down sooner than he had the slightest idea he could."[47]

On July 27, Baker set out from Bozeman with four companies of the 2nd Cavalry from Fort Ellis and four companies of the 7th Infantry from Fort

A drawing by A.R. Waud of the building of a railroad on the Great Plains, 1875. *Courtesy Library of Congress.*

Shaw under senior Captain Charles Rawn. The total force numbered over 350 officers and men, accompanied by 20 to 30 prospectors and wolfers, sixty-five military wagons and seven hundred animals. They made slow progress, as the Yellowstone was filled with late snow runoff and heavy spring rains. Although the plan had been to cross to the south bank, Baker decided to wait until they were farther downriver near Pompey's Pillar. On August 13, the expedition did not move, but a survey party advanced seven miles to the terminus of the previous year's survey and started work. It was calm in camp, and infantry Sergeant Fred Mischer wrote that the day "was spent by the command in trout fishing and necessary laundry labor."[48]

But unbeknownst to the expedition, eight hundred to one thousand Sioux warriors were headed upriver to raid the Crow; fortunately, they were on the other side of the Yellowstone. When their scouts discovered the Northern Pacific force about August 12, the temptation of the potentially large spoils in horses and cattle convinced them to attack the troops instead.[49] Unaware of the approaching enemy, Baker was unconcerned. Lieutenant James Bradley, of the 7th Infantry, explained the major's actions:

Main Street, Bozeman, Montana Territory, looking east, 1873. The town was named after John Bozeman, who established the Bozeman Trail and was one of the founders of the town in August 1864. *Courtesy Gallatin History Museum, Bozeman, Montana; Charles Rich Family Collection.*

Major Eugene M. Baker and officers at Fort Ellis, Montana, 1871. Major Baker is ninth from the left. Photograph by W.H. Jackson. *Courtesy the Montana Historical Society Research Center, Montana Historical Society, Helena, Montana.*

Troop F, 2nd Cavalry, at Fort Ellis, Montana Territory, 1867–72. *Courtesy the Montana Historical Society Research Center, Montana Historical Society, Helena, Montana.*

*The presence in the neighborhood of two or three Indian dogs had excited some apprehension that there were Indians about, but the general feeling was of confidence and security; and not only were no especial precautions taken by the commander of the force to guard against an attack, but upon the very night fixed for it he permitted himself to become unfitted for the proper performance of his duties by an over-indulgence in strong drink.*

*The camp was pitched upon ground favorable for defense, being located upon the margin of the stream, with a timbered slough sweeping in a semi-circular direction around it so as to form in connection with the river what may be termed an island of two or three score acres area, the whole at long rifle-range from the adjacent bluffs. To have rendered the position wholly secure, however, it would have been necessary so to guard the slough that it could not be occupied by the enemy as a preliminary to their attack; but this was not done. Fortunately it was rather the purpose of the Indians to get possession of the animals of the command with as little fighting as possible than to gain any decisive advantage over the troops, and their plans were laid accordingly.*[50]

Baker knew he had a favorable defensive position, and he posted a guard of twenty-six soldiers, commanded by officer of the guard Lieutenant William Logan of the 7th Infantry, to protect the cattle and mules. In the early hours of August 14, about three hundred Sioux warriors stealthily crossed the Yellowstone before Sitting Bull and the rest were ready. Baker settled down for an evening of poker and drinking. Officer of the day Captain Lewis Thompson of the cavalry made his round at 3:00 a.m. and found that all was peaceful.[51]

Yet the Indians were slowly infiltrating the army's position, coming first into contact with the prospectors and wolfers camped a short distance away. Sergeant John Ponsford of the 2nd Cavalry described what happened:

*There were some camp followers in the command, prospectors and wolfers, who made their beds and slept outside against a tree, but his* [Jack Gorman's] *cartridge and revolver were in the blanket with him. During the night (about 2:45 a.m.) he was lying awake and saw what he thought was a bunch of feathers moving and watching for a second or two found that the feathers had an Indian's head in them. He cocked his revolver and without moving his body shot the Indian through the head. The report of his pistol awoke the camp and the Indians commenced shooting at the soldiers but shot high.*[52]

Soon afterward, the Indians opened fire and advanced to capture the herd. At first the firing was thought to be caused by nervous sentries, but the war cries indicated that the Indians were indeed attacking in force.[53] Some of the officers were still playing poker, which had earlier included "the alcoholic Baker," "who took along a keg of whiskey when he finally retired to his tent."[54] According to Lieutenant Bradley's account of the battle, Captain Rawn realized what was happening and immediately

> *reported to Major Baker for orders and found him still in bed, stupefied with drink, skeptical as to the presence of an enemy, and inclined to treat the whole alarm as a groundless fright upon the part of the guard. It was difficult to get any order from him, but at last he directed... Captain Rawn to hold his men in camp; and, disgusted and angry, that officer returned to his command and upon his own responsibility deployed Companies E (Lieut. Reed) and G (Capt. Browning) in line on the lower side of the camp, facing the thicket in which the ambuscade had been formed...As bullets were flying freely through the camp, the remainder of the command was ordered to lie down in their company streets.*[55]

Although still skeptical of what was happening, Baker ordered Captain Thompson to assess the situation. Thompson almost lost his life by advancing past the sentries to determine the true nature of the fight and then reported to Major Baker, who finally ordered Captain Rawn to deploy his command. Rawn placed his two remaining companies in position so that his four infantry companies covered half the front, while the cavalry and citizens extended the line to the left, surrounding the camp. Sergeant Mischer noted:

> *Capt. Rawn, assuming charge of the infantry adopted a plan on the left that proved a good one and showed he had knowledge of his business. Giving orders to refrain from firing, he marched those companies to a point about 25 yards from camp and gave the command to lie down. Each remained in this position for what seemed like an age, but was probably not over 15 minutes...* [The Indians] *fired high and the war hoops plainly showed that a good sized band were before us, and that we were outnumbered four or five to one. Their aim was wild, as they fired over us every shot, and they showed no disposition to charge. As left guide the writer lay on the left of his company and frequently the balls would throw grass and mud into his face, as was noticed by Capt. Browning lying beside me, who remarked that they seemed to be firing lower.*[56]

With Baker incapacitated with drink, the courage and leadership of his subordinate officers and the fortitude and professionalism of the enlisted men eventually carried the day for the army.[57] The first exchanges ended at about 4:00 a.m., before both sides regrouped. As dawn approached, a group of infantry moved forward, noticed slight movement ahead of them and fired three volleys. The Indians broke and retreated to the heights.

As more Sioux crossed the river, Baker's numerical advantage disappeared, but the soldiers' defensive position was strong and protected them from most of the bullets. Stalemated and with limited options, in a show of courage, Sitting Bull took four of his warriors, walked down from the bluff, sat in plain view of the soldiers and smoked his pipe while bullets flew about them. Calmly finishing and cleaning his pipe, Sitting Bull and his companions walked back to the top of the bluff. Meanwhile, to demonstrate their bravery, Crazy Horse and White Bull mounted their ponies and raced in front of the soldiers. Crazy Horse's horse was hit, and White Bull carried him to safety.[58]

By 8:00 a.m., the Indians were gone, and reconnaissance by Captain Ball's cavalry company showed them in full retreat. The officers were anxious to follow the Indians, and Major Baker ordered Rawn to prepare two of his companies and announced his intention of taking them and two of his companies of cavalry to pursue the fleeing Sioux, but he soon forgot, changed his mind or returned to his whiskey. The Battle of Pryor's Creek, Baker's Battle, the Battle of Arrow Creek (the Indians' name) or the Battle of Poker Flats (Bradley's jocular name for it) was over. The army suffered one dead, Sergeant McLaren of the 7th Infantry, and three badly wounded privates. According to Lieutenant Bradley, more than one hundred Indian warriors were wounded and over forty killed, although all except three were carried from the field by the departing Indians.

General Winfield Scott Hancock (1824–1886). *Courtesy Library of Congress.*

A report of the battle reached Colonel Gibbon at Fort Shaw, and in his report to General Winfield

Scott Hancock in St. Paul, he wrote that had he been able to communicate to the men in the field, he would have placed Captain Rawn in command and had him arrest Major Baker.

In the following days, the expedition continued its slow march east along the north bank of the Yellowstone River, but engineer Hayden's fears of Indians and mistrust of Major Baker convinced him to insist—against the advice of his fellow surveyors and the pleas of the officers—on calling off the survey on August 20. They slowly surveyed a line northward to the Musselshell River and then westward toward the Missouri on their return. Shortly after Baker's return to post, on October 15, General Hancock had him arrested, but upon Hancock's replacement by General Alfred Terry, no charges were brought.[59] Even with Baker's lax leadership and drinking, Lieutenant Bradley lay the failure of the expedition entirely at the feet of Hayden, writing that a "great majority of the officers were eager to go on, to save the command from any suspicion of having been frightened from its purpose by Indian hostility."[60]

The 1873 expedition, under the leadership of Colonel David Stanley and Lieutenant Colonel George Custer, was twice the size of the 1872 expedition. The expense of this enormous expedition helped bankrupt the company and spark the Panic of 1873. Not until 1879 would construction of the Northern Pacific Railroad begin again under the leadership of Frederick Billings and Henry Villard, and the last spike was driven on September 8, 1883.[61]

But the frontier was only beginning to heat up, and the Battle of Pryor's Creek was a major precipitating factor in the coming Sioux War.

CHAPTER 5

# THE SIOUX WAR

The Sioux, an abbreviation of the Ojibway word *Nadousioux* (enemy), were arguably the most warlike and formidable Indian nation in the country. The Sioux "nation" consisted of the Lakota (Teton), Dakota (Santee) and Nakota (Yankton), who had migrated from Minnesota to the Great Plains in the late 1700s. They were allies with the equally warlike Northern Cheyenne.

The Lakota were the most powerful of the Sioux bands and consisted of the Sihasapa, Brule, Hunkpapa, Oglala, Sans Arc, Two Kettle and Minneconjou located in the area that would become South Dakota, Montana, Wyoming and Nebraska. Of these, the Brule and Oglala were the most aggressive, and their homeland was in the Black Hills, a sacred place where the spirits dwelled. Red Cloud (1822–1909) and Crazy Horse (1842–1877) were Oglala; Sitting Bull (1831–1890) was a Hunkpapa.[62]

The Indian way of warfare focused on lightning raids, ambushes and brief skirmishes. There was generally no coordination, organized strategy or tactics as each warrior fought for himself. Preparations for battle would be elaborate and ritualistic, and victory dances and ceremonies would follow successful battles. Raiding and harassment were regarded as sport, and a sustained battle could be disastrous; if the attackers felt they were losing, they would flee, particularly if their camp was threatened. The art of Indian warfare was to attack suddenly, create confusion, drive away or kill the enemy and plunder the spoils. In serious fights, no prisoners would be taken and the wounded enemy would be killed. The most vicious practice feared by white men—scalping—was a sign of victory and a badge of honor. Since the spirit is located in the hair, it was believed scalping prevented the victim from entering the afterlife.

Sitting Bull (circa 1831–1890), leader of the Hunkpapa Sioux, 1881. *Courtesy Library of Congress.*

This type of warfare infuriated the military, whose leaders had been trained in "civilized" tactics from the Mexican War through the Civil War. Suddenly, to be successful they had to adopt Indian tactics like sudden attacks on unsuspecting villages while they exploited their advantages of superior fire power, weapons, supplies, organization and communication. Due to the nature of the army, leaders were also willing to accept greater casualties because there were always new recruits, and they were willing to engage in not only winter war but total war. Destroying villages destroyed the Indians' food, shelter and horses and exposed the survivors to the elements. Flags of truce were not recognized, women and children were expendable and possessions were destroyed because, while cruel and inhuman, it forced peace sooner.[63]

The cataclysmic collision of the two forces manifested itself in the Sioux War of 1876.

The 1868 Treaty of Fort Laramie had forbidden whites from the sacred Black Hills area, but rumors of gold brought in prospectors, and by 1874, the situation had become critical. In May 1874, a force under Lieutenant Colonel George Custer entered the area, ostensibly to build a fort but in reality to ascertain if there was gold present. The presence of gold was confirmed; therefore, the Indians would have to leave as white prospectors and settlers started to stream in. Meanwhile, more and more Indians were leaving the area amid white depredations to join the Sioux forces off the reservation.

In May 1875, a Sioux delegation went to Washington, D.C., in an unsuccessful attempt to persuade the government to live up to the promises of the treaty. Later that year, the government sent out commissions to each of the Indian agencies in a futile attempt to gain support for a new treaty turning the Black Hills over to the whites. Years of frustration on both sides were making a peaceful settlement impossible. The Sioux had raided around the periphery of the unceded territory, terrorized friendly tribes, contested the development of the Northern Pacific Railroad, disrupted the management of the reservation and interfered with the exploitation of the Black Hills. The whites had been encroaching on the reservation for years, invaded the Black Hills, taken over the traditional hunting grounds in Montana and been fighting skirmishes with the Indians for years. After the government reached its foregone decision, runners were sent to the roaming Sioux to tell them that they had to move to the reservation by January 31, 1876, or be certified as hostile.

When the deadline passed, the problem was turned over to the army, and on February 8, 1876, General Sheridan, commander of the Department of the Missouri, sent word to Brigadier General George Crook, commander of the Department of the Platte, and Brigadier General Alfred Terry, commander of the Department of Dakota, to launch a winter campaign against the hostiles. It is estimated that perhaps 5,500 Sioux were off the reservation with about 1,500 Northern Cheyenne and Arapaho allies, including up to 2,000 warriors. With the advantages of mobility and knowledge of the area, the Indians were ready to take a stand.

The army plan was to use three independent units—the Montana Column, Dakota Column and Wyoming Column—to surround the Indians and force them onto the reservation. General Crook headed the Wyoming Column and left Fort Fetterman in early February, hoping to reach Crazy Horse's or Sitting Bull's villages while they were in winter camp. A bitter march through the cold and snows of February and March culminated in an attack on a Cheyenne village near the Powder River in southeastern Montana. The Cheyenne mounted an unexpectedly stiff defense and, in pursuing the army, recaptured most of the horses that had been stolen in the attack. The Wyoming Column limped back into Fort Fetterman on March 26. With the Dakota Column snowbound at Fort Abraham Lincoln, only the Montana Column was on the move.[64]

On March 17, Colonel John Gibbon's infantry left Fort Shaw for Fort Ellis under the command of Captain Rawn. The column had to march through bitter cold and snow several inches deep. On Sunday, March 19, Rawn became seriously snowblind and turned command over to Captain Freeman. Lieutenant James Bradley related what snowblindness felt like:

*Left*: General George Crook (1830–1890), circa 1875. *Courtesy Library of Congress.*

*Below*: Major General Philip Sheridan (1831–1888), 1861. *Courtesy Library of Congress.*

> *The loss of sight comes on with a feeling such as is created by smoke in the eyes, that, if the case is a severe one, soon increases into the most intense burning pain. The eyes cannot bear the light and the eyeballs seem to roll in liquid fire with a grating feeling as though in contact with particles of sand. The temptation to bandage them or apply water is great, but should be resisted, as the one heats the eyes and the other increases the irritation, and the pain is only intensified.*[65]

On March 20, Rawn found himself completely incapacitated and returned to Fort Shaw for treatment. He tried to rejoin the column when his condition improved but suffered a relapse at Fort Ellis and finally returned to Fort Shaw.[66]

On March 28, the Montana Column reached Fort Ellis and resumed its march to the Yellowstone on March 30, while the Fort Ellis cavalry prepared to follow. The plan was to cooperate with Crook's Wyoming Column by going to the Yellowstone River, down the Bozeman Trail, to the valleys of the Little Bighorn, Rosebud Creek and Tongue River. The force consisted of 233 officers and men of the 7th Infantry. On April 1, Colonel Gibbon joined them with 198 troopers from the 2nd Cavalry. Cold weather and heavy snows held the column to sixteen to nineteen miles each day. Moving east, with Lieutenant Bradley's scouts in the lead, they learned that the Wyoming Column was not taking to the field and that both Crook and the Dakota Column under Lieutenant Colonel George Custer did not expect to move from their posts until May. General Terry ordered the Montana Column to temporarily stop at Fort Pease, an abandoned trading post. They stopped again from May 14 through 19 on Little Porcupine Creek and then moved east to opposite the mouth of Rosebud Creek, where they stayed until June 5.

As Gibbon concentrated his forces at the mouths of the Rosebud and Tongue Rivers, the Wyoming Column finally left Fort Fetterman and the Dakota Column left Fort Abraham Lincoln. On June 10, Gibbon arrived at the Powder River and met with General Terry and Lieutenant Colonel Custer aboard the supply steamboat *Far West* to plan strategy. Gibbon was ordered to return to the Montana Column and keep it at the mouth of Rosebud Creek.

While the armies were moving, the combined village of Sitting Bull, Crazy Horse, Old Bull and others was situated on the lower Rosebud, holding its sacred Sun Dance prior to the summer hunt. This was perhaps the largest gathering of Native Americans ever in the United States, and

*Left*: Photographic portrait of (Brevet) General John Gibbon (1827–1896), by D.F. Barry; no date. *Courtesy the Montana Historical Society Research Center, Montana Historical Society, Helena, Montana.*

*Right*: General Alfred Terry (1827–1890), circa 1868. *Courtesy Library of Congress.*

on June 14, the village moved to the Little Bighorn River. News reached them that General Crook's troops were approaching, but the Indian victory at the Battle of Rosebud Creek on June 17 protected the large combined Sioux and Cheyenne village and removed the Wyoming Column from the equation as Crook's column withdrew to awaited reinforcements.[67]

The plan developed on the *Far West* called for Custer's Dakota Column to go up the Rosebud and drive down the Little Bighorn from the south; Gibbon's Montana Column would be ferried across the Yellowstone, ascend the Bighorn and enter the Little Bighorn from the north; Custer was expected to strike the blow, but not before Gibbon was positioned to block any escape. Gibbon estimated that he could be in place by June 26.

On June 22, Custer led his cavalry up the Rosebud. Terry's plan called for Custer to continue up the Rosebud, but Custer followed the divide between the Rosebud and the Little Bighorn. At dawn on June 25, Custer's Arikara and Crow scouts spotted the Sioux and Cheyenne village fifteen miles away. Although Custer could not see the village, he feared that the Indians had discovered him and would flee, so he ordered an attack at once. Three companies under Captain Frederick Benteen were held as battalion reserve, tasked with protecting the pack train, and were behind Custer and Major Marcus Reno. Three companies under Major Reno attacked the southern end of the village while Custer attacked the far end. Due to the size of the village and distances involved, Reno was routed before Custer reached the middle of the village. Hunkpapa Chief Gall led the Indians across the river from the center of the village and drove Custer's men back to the high ridge downstream as Crazy Horse's forces circled below the village and closed on Custer from the north. Within one hour, Custer and his five companies were annihilated while Reno's disorganized survivors fled to a hill on the bluffs above the river where they were soon joined by Benteen's three companies and the pack train. Benteen's men helped form a defensive line to protect Reno's shattered command, saving them from annihilation.

It was a battle the Indians would never fight again. Never before or after were they better prepared, more numerous than the enemy, united and confident, superbly led, emotionally charged to defend their homeland and freedom and able to catch the army in an unfavorable tactical situation.[68]

Lithograph of Lieutenant Colonel George Custer's death struggle at the Battle of the Little Big Horn, by S.H. Redmond. Lithograph produced by Britton, Rey & Co., San Francisco. *Courtesy Library of Congress.*

While this was going on, General Terry's command moved upstream to the Bighorn and up the Little Bighorn without incident. On June 27, it set off with Lieutenant Bradley and the scouts in the lead. "The troopers cautiously guided their horses forward past burial tipis, coming upon several beheaded and mutilated bodies of white men and then the heads of three whites hanging from a lodgepole, hair burned away, unrecognizable. Articles of soldiers' clothing lay all around, bloodstained and bullet-pierced."[69] Lieutenant Bradley wrote:

> *Of the 206 bodies buried on the field, there were very few that I did not see, and beyond scalping, in possibly a majority of cases, there was little mutilation. Many of the bodies were not even scalped, and in the comparatively few cases of disfiguration, it appeared to me the result rather of a blow with a knife, hatchet or war club to finish a wounded man, than a deliberate mutilation. Many of Custer's men must have been disabled with wounds during the fight, and when the savages gained possession of the field such would probably be mainly killed in the manner indicated...*
>
> *The real mutilation occurred in the case of Reno's men, who had fallen near the village. These had been visited by the squaws and children, and in some instances the bodies were frightfully butchered. Fortunately not many were exposed to such a fate. Custer's field was some distance from the village, and appears not to have been visited by these hags, which probably explains the exemption from mutilation of those who had fallen there.*[70]

Unable to continue staying together in one large group, the Indians began to split up into bands for the summer hunt and to escape the pursuing army. General Crook took to the field but failed to find any large group of Indians, and orders from General Sheridan committed Terry to establish a cantonment on the Yellowstone at the mouth of the Tongue River, with Colonel Nelson Miles in command, while Terry reported to St. Paul headquarters.

Meanwhile, Crook's search took him outside Montana, and after weeks of pointless searching, on September 9, an advance company finally found a small Sioux village at Slim Buttes, which they attacked and destroyed. Crook's column disbanded when they reached Camp Robinson.

With autumn coming, Colonel Miles took to the field with more than one thousand troops from the new Tongue River Cantonment. He quickly responded to Sioux attacks on wagons carrying supplies to the new fort, and on October 30, he found Sitting Bull's village on Cedar Creek. The two soldiers met. Sitting Bull demanded that the soldiers leave the unceded land and maintained that his people simply wanted to be left alone; Miles demanded their immediate surrender. After the talks ended, a skirmish broke out as the Indians attempted to set the grass on fire. The soldiers broke the Indian line, and the Sioux abandoned their village and fled. Sitting Bull and thirty families escaped toward the Missouri River, while some other groups began returning to the reservation.

Miles returned briefly to the fort to re-equip before pursuing Sitting Bull, catching up with the Sioux on Ash Creek on December 14. Although the village contained over one hundred lodges, most of the men were out hunting when the howitzer started firing and the soldiers attacked. The Hunkpapa Sioux abandoned their village, rode south to find help at an Oglala village and then headed north to start their long trek to Canada.

With Sitting Bull weakened, the army focused on Crazy Horse and his village below the Yellowstone River in southeastern Montana. By late November, as the Sioux began to regroup after the summer hunt, Crazy Horse's village numbered about 250 lodges, with about 500 more to arrive. With winter on the way, the Indians decided to talk to Miles about surrendering, but Miles's Crow scouts fired on the supplicants. Crazy Horse

Crazy Horse (circa 1840–1877) and his band of Indians on their way from Camp Sheridan to surrender to General Crook at the Red Cloud Agency. Berghavy, from sketches by Mr. Hottes, 1877. *Courtesy Library of Congress.*

soon organized a series of raids on the fort and its suppliers in response. Miles took to the field, but Crazy Horse was ready and attacked in the falling snow on January 8. The Battle of Wolf Mountain saw fierce fighting, but the army's artillery and the developing blizzard forced the Indians to withdraw.

In February, Miles negotiated the surrender of the Cheyenne and Crow, but when they learned of better surrender terms at the reservation, they chose to go there, and General Crook received the credit for their surrender. Miles returned to the field in April to search for Lame Deer's village, finally locating it on Muddy Creek. The attack commenced on May 7, and Miles ordered his soldiers not to shoot the women and children fleeing the camp. As soon as the firing started, Chief Lame Deer was pointed out to Miles, who ordered a cease-fire to meet with the chief. In the confusion, Lame Deer picked up his cocked rifle and fired at Miles but killed his orderly instead. In moments, Lame Deer was dead, and the battle continued until the soldiers flanked the Indians.

The Sioux War was over, with most of the non-treaty Indians on the reservation or in Canada with Sitting Bull. The Tongue River Cantonment became Fort Keogh with Colonel Miles in charge.[71]

Montana seemed at peace, unaware that more trouble was on the way from a most unlikely direction.

CHAPTER 6

# A FORT FOR MISSOULA

With the Sioux War over, life returned to normal for the 7th Infantry in Montana. The officers and men settled back into routine: escorting Indian delegations, scouting, protecting supply trains, repairing telegraph lines, constructing and repairing roads and forts, maintaining discipline, tracking down deserters, helping local enforcement with criminals, maintaining drill proficiency and monitoring the Indian tribes for potential problems. But 217 miles to the southwest of Fort Shaw, headquarters of the 7th Infantry, the citizens of the small frontier town of Missoula were getting nervous.

Founded in 1860 as Hellgate Village, the town of Missoula was growing and was feeling anxious without any army protection in the area. Captain Christopher P. Higgins had resigned from the military in 1860; bought Mr. Isaac's interest in the Worden and Isaac's mercantile in Walla Walla, Washington; and convinced his new partner, Francis Worden, to move to the Missoula Valley. Earlier, Higgins had been a trusted member of Governor Isaac Stevens's Expedition of 1853–55, which had explored the area and made peace with the Indian tribes in the region as Stevens prepared to assume his duties as governor of the new Washington Territory. While in the Missoula Valley, Higgins saw the potential of the area to become an economic hub for the entire western portion of what would become Montana. In June 1860, Higgins, Worden and their clerk, Frank Woody, who had spent a year in the Missoula Valley in 1856–57, left Walla Walla with a permit to trade with the Indians and a pack train of seventy-six animals piled high with merchandise. Their first store was located in a tent, but they soon arranged with David Pattee, an 1858 settler in the Bitterroot Valley, to construct a sixteen- by eighteen-foot log structure with a sod roof to house their establishment.

The little town of Hellgate Village had a short, brief and violent history, in part tied to the activities of the Vigilantes of Virginia City, who executed six men in the area with ties to Sheriff Plummer's band of road agents. But despite the rough nature of life in western Montana, Higgins's dream was becoming a reality as the little town started to prosper, spurred by the discovery of gold in the Cedar Creek and Gold Creek areas.

In November 1864, Higgins, Worden and Pattee formed the Missoula Mills Company. They moved four miles upstream from Hellgate Village and constructed a sawmill near the mouth of Rattlesnake Creek after it joins the Clark's Fork of the Columbia River. In the spring of 1865, they built a flour mill and moved their store from Hellgate Village. The new store was a two-story building with the upper floor used as a Masonic hall, courtroom and entertainment center for the community. That same year, two hotels, a carpenter shop and several log homes were built. The following year, Edward Bonner and David Welch arrived with 125 pack animals to build a store to compete with the Missoula Mills store. This was the beginning of what would become the Missoula Mercantile, which under the later leadership of Andrew Hammond dominated western Montana for nearly a century. Within several years, Hellgate Village disappeared as development centered on Missoula.[72] With the growth of the economy, population numbers grew; the census of 1870 listed the population of Missoula at 400 out of a total territorial population of 20,595.

The founding fathers of Missoula had a greater vision, and they knew the value of obtaining a fort for their new community; the US Army has always proven to be an economic engine for whatever community in which it is situated. There was also real fear of Indian attack, for even though the local Salish, Kootenai and Pend d'Oreille Indians (known collectively as the Flathead Indians) were peaceful, there was the occasional raid, and the threat of depredation by the Blackfeet Nation to the north, the Sioux and Cheyenne to the east and the Nez Perce traveling through the area every year from the west meant that there was reason to be concerned. Additionally, the February 5, 1874 "Memorial of the Legislature of Montana Territory" to the Forty-third Congress listed concerns with the Cayuse, Coeur d'Alene, Klikitat, Yakima, Walla-Walla, Spokane, Colville, Kettle Indians and stragglers from the Modoc tribe. It also went on to bemoan the clandestine

Front Street, Missoula, 1874. *Courtesy Archives and Special Collections, Mansfield Library, University of Montana.*

sale of "spirituous liquors" to the Indians "by lawless white persons and half-breeds, arousing all their bad passions."

As early as 1871, Missoula citizens sought a fort for their protection. Petitions from territorial governor Benjamin Potts were sent to Congress, and Montana's territorial legislative delegate to Congress, Martin Maginnis, lobbied in the halls of Washington. Finally, in 1876, their efforts were rewarded, and Lieutenant Colonel Wesley Merritt, of the 9th Cavalry, was sent to the area and, after being wined and dined, determined that there was a need for a one- or two-company post at or near Hellgate Pass. Commander of the Military Division of the Missouri Lieutenant General Sheridan concurred, and President Grant approved the recommendation.

Later that year, Lieutenant Colonel Charles Gilbert and acting engineer Second Lieutenant Charles Worden of the 7th Infantry arrived to determine a site for the new fort. Forgoing the proposed Blackfoot bridge and Grant Creek sites, they decided that the Bitterroot River location, four miles west of town, was the best spot for the new fort. At an elevation of 3,400 feet and located on a large flat surrounded by mountains, the new post had not only a great defensive location but a healthy one as well. Fifteen miles to the southwest was Lolo Mountain, one of the highest peaks of the Bitterroot

First Higgins Avenue Bridge, Missoula, 1874. *Courtesy Archives and Special Collections, Mansfield Library, University of Montana.*

Missoula from Waterworks Hill, 1876. *Courtesy Archives and Special Collections, Mansfield Library, University of Montana.*

Mountains, and the fertile valley of the Bitterroot River stretched sixty miles southward from the new fort. Lieutenant Worden proceeded to lay out the military reservation, and the county surveyor was called upon to determine the limits of the post. In May 1877, the quartermaster general remitted $20,000 to the chief quartermaster of the Department of Dakota for the construction of the new post.[73]

On June 5, 1877, Colonel Gibbon ordered his senior captain, Charles Rawn, to take his Company I and Captain William Logan's Company A, numbering six officers and sixty-seven enlisted men, to Missoula.[74] Rawn's company was to garrison the new fort while Logan's company was to help construct the fort before returning to Fort Shaw. On June 9, the two companies left Fort Shaw with the wives and children of the officers and noncommissioned officers, as well as the company laundresses. Accompanying Rawn was his wife, Isabel, who would give birth to their first daughter, Margaret, on August 16. (By that time, Rawn was doing battle with the Nez Perce Indians, so he made prior arrangements with Dr. Emil Hsukr to attend Isabel at her confinement.)[75] Following the Mullan Military Road, the column traveled 217 miles in seventeen days, suffering through wet weather and muddy road conditions before arriving in Missoula.

Fort Missoula along the Bitterroot River, with Missoula at far left, circa 1890. *Courtesy Stan Cohen.*

The Fort Missoula Powder Magazine, built in 1878, was constructed with mortar and fieldstones and used to store explosives when the fort was active. The small building was built along the river, close enough for easy access but far enough away to minimize danger from explosions. *Courtesy Stan Cohen.*

Rawn and Acting Assistant Quartermaster Lieutenant Johnson left the command at a place they called "Frenchwoman's" on June 12 to go to Helena to start negotiating contracts for necessary supplies. The position of acting assistant quartermaster was one of the numerous logistical and administrative duties given to junior officers in the absence of higher-ranking officers specializing in support positions. Rawn left the lieutenant to complete matters as he hurried to Missoula, arriving on June 19. Upon his arrival, he stayed at the Kennedy House and was fêted by leaders of the community while he started soliciting local businessmen for necessary goods and services.[76]

On June 25, the two companies of the 7th Infantry arrived in two columns, led by fife and drum. Corporal Charles Loynes wrote, "On a beautiful June day we entered the struggling village of Missoula, composed at the time of a gristmill, about twenty log houses, and a camp of two or three hundred friendly Indians under an old chief about eighty years of age by the name of Big Canoe."[77] The men marched through Missoula, crossed the Clark's Fork River and made their way to the site of the proposed fort, where they pitched their tents and started work.[78]

The entrance to Fort Missoula with officers' row on the left, circa 1890. *Courtesy Stan Cohen.*

Officers' row at Fort Missoula, 1912–15. *Courtesy the HMFM Robert Dwaine Siperly Collection (1993.033), used by permission of the Historical Museum at Fort Missoula.* 

Although the work of construction began immediately, the lack of equipment, the long distance that lumber had to be hauled and the shortage of labor made progress slow. Captain Rawn wrote to the assistant adjutant general for the Department of Dakota in St. Paul:

> *Immediately after my arrival here the work of building the post commenced and considering the few men of the troops who could render any assistance as mechanics and the fact that the necessary lumber had to be procured several miles from the garrison and then only in such quantities as a small saw-mill could cut it, together with other causes which will be given hereafter in this communication, the work of erection has progressed as rapidly as could, under the circumstances be expected.*[79]

Rawn wrote again to the assistant adjutant general on July 13:

> *Understanding that Privates Stivers and Devoss of Company I, 7th Infantry are now at Fort Shaw, I respectfully request that they be ordered to report to their company for duty. At once. The men at this command are very heavily tasked at present going on guard with only one night in bed, and doing heavy fatigue duty every other day. I am informed that Private Stivers is a very expert axeman, and that Devoss is a stone-mason. Both of them therefore are men whose services are very much needed here especially Devoss, as there is no one in the command who understands the masons trade.*[80]

The progress of constructing Fort Missoula was greatly delayed when the garrison was first detailed to try to stop the invading Nez Perce at Lolo Canyon in July and then battle the Indians at the Battle of the Big Hole in early August. It was not until the return to Missoula of four companies under the command of Captain Rawn on August 21 that construction resumed. In his September 30 report to the assistant adjutant general, Rawn stated that the officers' quarters and company quarters were under good headway and the commissary and quartermaster's storehouse had already been used for storing supplies. Additionally, a large cellar was being dug to preserve such articles of subsistence that might be injured by the frost. He went on to write that a "corral had been partly completed, in fact considering the hard-ships the troops have undergone, the Indian campaigns, and the skeleton strength of the Companies, I am well pleased with the progress made in the construction of the new post."[81]

Ordnance storehouse and log living quarters at Fort Missoula, circa 1900. *Courtesy the HMFM Rev. John McCarthy Collection (1983.056), used by permission of the Historical Museum at Fort Missoula. All rights reserved.*

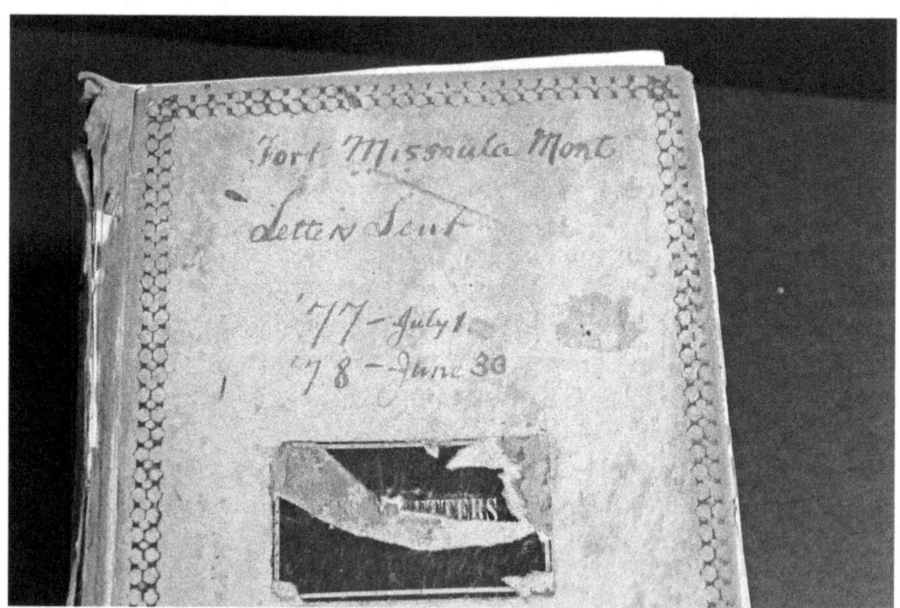


Leather journal of Fort Missoula letters, July 1, 1877–June 30, 1878. *Courtesy the HMFM Ed W. Radloff Collection (1990.049), used by permission of the Historical Museum at Fort Missoula. All rights reserved.*

Rawn was also confronted with the problem of deserters. Many men joined the army to stay warm and be fed during the winter, and when spring and summer arrived, many of them simply left. At one point, Rawn informed the Missoula sheriff: "Sir: Please find enclosed description of two men who deserted last night from Company 'J' 7th Infantry. They are supposed to have gone down the river in a small boat; they have taken their Guns, Blankets. If captured a reward of $30. for each will be paid for them, as soon as Congress makes an appropriation."[82]

In September 1877, General Sherman visited the area. His impression of the fort was favorable, and in his report, he suggested that it be enlarged. He wrote to the secretary of war that he would furnish Captain Rawn with "a modified plan, and send a copy of it to General Sheridan. I regard Missoula as a strategic point that will remain forever, made so by the conformation of the rivers and mountains. These will force all roads to converge here, and four hundred men here will equal a thousand at any point within 400 miles." He also noted that "had there been four companies here last year the Nez Perces would not have dared to revolt."[83] The post was enlarged to garrison four companies, construction quickened and on November 8 the post was officially named Fort Missoula. On November 14, Captain Rawn and the 7th Infantry were replaced by Lieutenant Colonel John Brooke and four companies of the 3rd Infantry.[84]

Rawn and his men were greatly relieved to be returning to Fort Shaw after the devastating consequences of their participation in the surprising and unanticipated Nez Perce War.

CHAPTER 7

# THE NEZ PERCE, PART I

For over ten thousand years, the Nez Perce Indians had lived peacefully in the area where Idaho, Oregon and Washington converge. They were friendly to the white man from the beginning, even helping the Lewis and Clark Expedition avoid disaster, and they were always proud that they had never shed white man's blood. Then came 1877.

The place they called home was a land of wide-open spaces—a high plateau cut into precipitous cliffs and valleys, estimated to be 13.5 million acres. It was a land passed over by the first white settlers on their way to the lush and fertile Willamette Valley located between two imposing mountain ranges: the Oregon Coast Range to the west and the Cascade Range to the east. The four to six thousand Nez Perce ranged widely and freely in the hills and valleys to the east, between the Cascades and the Rockies. The land provided them subsistence, affluence, liberty and power. As with all Indian tribes, they did not own the land but shared a communal and spiritual relationship with it. The various bands were also bound by a common language, a sacred history and shared ceremonials. But as the western coastal areas of the Pacific Northwest became overpopulated, whites began to see the desirability of the region and started to move in.[85]

Nez Perce contact with the whites followed the traditional pattern. Mountain men followed quickly behind Lewis and Clark and were tolerated. The missionaries came soon thereafter. Presbyterian missionary Henry Spaulding went to the Nez Perce in response to their request for teachers and textbooks. Settling near Lapwai Creek in 1836, he immediately began interfering with local governance. Spaulding and medical missionary Elijah White began to introduce new laws to serve their interests. These laws, delivered to the tribe in 1842, violated the Nez Perce civil rights, shifted political power to the federal government, supported the change to an agrarian economy and introduced the concept of a centralized head chief speaking for the majority. The tribe split; one group tried to adapt to the white man's ways while the other tried desperately to remain loyal to their traditions.[86]

To systemize relationships and preserve the peace, the federal government first negotiated a treaty in 1855 that reduced the Nez Perce land by thirteen million acres; codified the Christian laws; provided federal payments, surveys and roadways; vowed to preserve friendly relationships; allotted individual farms and punished those who left them; and created the position of head chief. Chief Lawyer, bilingual and Christian, was recognized as the head chief by the federal government, although not by his fellow chiefs. He was paid $500 a year and provided with a comfortable home and ten acres of plowed and fenced land.

This treaty, like most, was not destined to last long. In 1860, gold was discovered on the reservation, and thousands of prospectors and settlers began pouring into land guaranteed to the Nez Perce. The subsequent "Thief Treaty" of 1863 cost the Nez Perce $3 million worth of gold (reimbursed by the federal government in 1960) and approximately six million more acres of land. The concepts of head chief and majority rule were maintained as the government held that since the signatories represented a majority, the treaty bound all of the bands. Five bands refused to accept this treaty, turned down all federal payments and benefits and invested no authority in the concepts of head chief or majority rule.

Of the five non-treaty Nez Perce bands, Old Chief Joseph was the leader of the Wallowa Band. He had been one of the first Christian converts and had helped establish the original reservation in 1855 in exchange for an assurance that whites would never settle in the sacred Wallowa Valley. However, feeling deceived by the 1863 treaty, he condemned it, declared the sale of the Wallowa as illegal, destroyed his flag, renounced Christianity and refused to move from the valley. Upon his death in 1871, his son Young Joseph became chief. Of the other bands, Chief Looking Glass led the Alpowai, White Bird was chief and shaman of the Lahmtahma, Husus Kute and Hahtalekin led the Palus from the Lower Snake River and Toohoolhoolzote was chief of those from the high country between the Salmon and Snake Rivers.

Chief Joseph (1840–1904); no date. *Courtesy Library of Congress.*

When the US government attempted a compromise favoring the Nez Perce in 1872, it failed in the face of opposition of the western politicians, especially Oregon governor Lafayette Grover. With settlers pouring in and no federal protection, traditional nomadic life became unsustainable, and something had to be done.

In 1874, General Oliver Otis Howard became commander of the Department of the Columbia. Howard was a very pious and devout man, had been an excellent general during the Civil War, lost his right arm at the Battle of Fair Oaks (for which he was awarded a Medal of Honor), returned to fight in many battles and commanded two corps during Sherman's March to the Sea. After the war, he became commissioner of the Bureau of Freedmen and Refugees and founded Howard University for freed blacks before commanding troops against the Apache.[87] He was known as the "Christian General" and the "One-Armed General." However, like most general officers who had learned their lessons during the Mexican War and the Civil War, he was not prepared for what was coming, and he would be outmaneuvered and outfought by the Nez Perce, whose nickname for him was "General Day-After-Tomorrow Howard" because he was late for everything.

Howard met with the Nez Perce in Lapwai in November 1876. Joseph reiterated the position of the non-treaty Nez Perce, but Howard told them to either move to the reservation or be moved. When Toohoolhoolzote spoke dramatically and at length about their rights and religion, Howard lost his temper and temporarily arrested him, fearing a repeat of the murder of peace commissioners by the Modoc Indians several years before. At another council on May 14, the Nez Perce leaders tried to change Howard's mind, but to no avail, and on May 15, facing the inevitable, they set off for their homes to start packing. On May 21, General Howard, confident that the situation had been resolved, telegraphed the War Department that all was in order, the non-treaty Nez Perce were aware of the thirty-day notice and his troops were standing by.[88] To the Nez Perce, he said that if they were not on the reservation on time, "I shall consider that you want to fight, and will send my soldiers to drive you on."[89]

Major General Oliver O. Howard (1830–1909), circa 1860. *Courtesy Library of Congress.*

Joseph returned to the Wallowa Valley, and despite the fact that many of his warriors wanted war, he convinced them to move to the reservation and they started gathering their livestock in preparation for the move. As Joseph wrote, "There was a great deal of war talk and a great deal of excitement. There was one young warrior present whose father, Eagle Robe, had been killed by a white man five years before. This man's blood was bad against white men, and he left the council calling for revenge."[90]

As Joseph continued to counsel for peace, on June 14, this warrior, Wahlitits (Shore Crossing), and his "hot-blooded" friends Red Moccasin Tops and Swan Necklace left camp and killed four white men who were notorious for their ill treatment of the Indians. Upon their return to camp, Wahlitits's deed was celebrated and a larger war party was formed; by the next day, eleven more whites had been killed. Joseph lamented:

> *If General Howard had given me plenty of time to gather up my stock and had treated Too-hool-hool-sote as a man should be treated, there would have been no war. My friends among white men have blamed me for the war. I am not to blame. When my young men began the killing, my heart was hurt. Although I did not justify them, I remembered all the insults I had endured, and my blood was on fire.*[91]

As the army left Fort Lapwai to restore order, Joseph's band moved sixteen miles away to White Bird Creek, where Chief White Bird was already encamped. On June 17, a force of ninety-nine soldiers and eleven volunteers under Captain David Perry fired on a Nez Perce party under a flag of truce. Perry had fallen into a perfect trap set by White Bird. With the Indians displaying skill, cunning, strategy and great leadership, the result was a disaster for the army and volunteers as they suffered thirty-four killed while wounding only a few Indians.

Embarrassed by this loss and acting on false information that Chief Looking Glass was helping the hostiles, General Howard ordered Captain Steven Whipple to arrest the chief. Looking Glass consistently maintained his innocence and had already moved his band to the Lapwai Reservation when the force under Whipple attacked the sleeping village on July 1. Looking Glass and his band fled and joined the other hostiles, where Looking Glass assumed leadership as the great warrior chief. Looking Glass stated:

> *I have been treated worse than a dog by the very same Army that was once a friend. My father's warriors fought many battles as allies of the United*

*The Idaho Indian War*, Chas. W. Phillip, photographer, Walla Walla, 1877. Identified by historian/author Bill Gulick as (left to right) Billy Carter, Ollokot (Chief Joseph's brother) and Middle Bear. *Courtesy Library of Congress.*

> *States soldiers... We had friends and relations killed in fighting along with the United States troops...Now, my people, as long as I live I will never make peace with the treacherous Americans.*[92]

Chief Looking Glass (1832–1877); no date. *Courtesy National Anthropological Archives, Smithsonian Institution [NAA INV 01005001].*

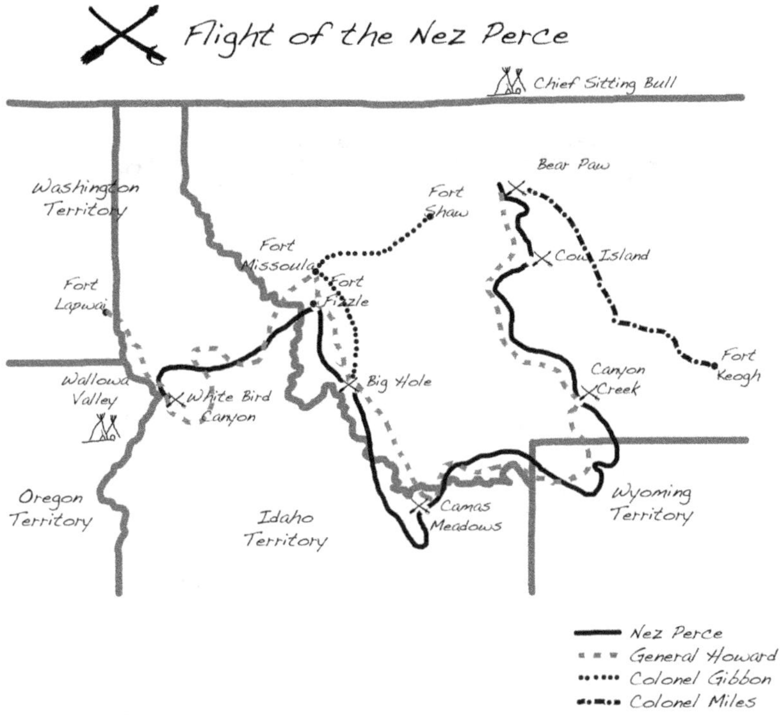


Map of the 1877 flight of the Nez Perce. *Courtesy Bryan Steward, artist, 2015.*

During the next month, Howard gathered his forces. Skirmishes along the Cottonwood on July 3–5 were followed, on July 11, by a battle near the Clearwater River in Idaho. A dozen soldiers were killed as the two hundred troopers were besieged for two days before the Nez Perce once again slipped away, forced to leave much of their supplies behind.

While Howard dallied, the Nez Perce met in council on July 15. Joseph argued against moving out of their homeland, although he suggested the possibility of joining their friends the Flatheads. Looking Glass argued for traveling east to the plains of Montana, where they could obtain aid from their friends the Crow. With White Bird acting as mediator, Looking Glass's plan was adopted.[93]

The Nez Perce headed for the old Nez Perce Trail, used by Lewis and Clark, over Lolo Pass to the Bitterroot Valley. In their way stood a small little fort just barely under construction.

CHAPTER *8*

# ENCOUNTER IN LOLO CANYON

Even though the Nez Perce were leaving his jurisdiction, the War Department gave General Howard overall command of the operation. As he gathered 700 men and started for the Lolo Trail, he alerted the troops in Montana that the Nez Perce were headed in their direction and told them to stop the Indians at the east end of Lolo Trail. Then, waiting until July 30 to start pursuit, and aided by a company of axemen from Lewiston, Howard took nine days to cross the mountains. Meanwhile, the Nez Perce had started their descent into Montana on July 25, with an estimated 300 warriors and 450 women and children.[94]

Aware of the danger as early as July 4, Colonel Gibbon telegraphed Captain Rawn at Fort Missoula via Deer Lodge: "Send me by telegraph the first authentic intelligence from Indians west of you." Without telegraph service in Missoula, all messages were sent to Deer Lodge and then forwarded by mail courier.[95] Gibbon then proceeded to order reinforcements for Rawn from Fort Ellis as he prepared to take the field with his Fort Shaw troops.

Meanwhile, Rawn was alone in Missoula.

To protect his flanks, on July 16, Rawn and Indian agent Major Peter Ronan went to the Flathead Reservation to meet with Chief Andrea of the Pend d'Oreilles and Chief Arlee of the treaty Salish (who had accepted the Treaty of 1855 and moved to the Jocko Valley Reservation) to protect his northern and western flank. He found that despite their traditional friendship with the Nez Perce, they felt that their current interests required them to maintain friendship with the white man. They were peacefully and firmly established on a reservation rich in land and horses and did not wish trouble. They even had an organized police force of thirty warriors to keep the peace. When Rawn asked if they could supply scouts, they said that they were willing but only if Rawn would pay them and provide them with uniforms. Authorized to provide uniforms but not pay, Rawn declined, and no scouts were forthcoming.

The next day, Rawn visited non-treaty Salish chief Charlo (who had not accepted the 1855 treaty) in the Bitterroot Valley to protect his southern flank. In his letterbook, Rawn recorded Charlo's response:

> *In answer to an inquiry as to the feelings of his people he replied in* [effect] *the same as the Indians of the agency, and after a eulogy upon his father Victor an Indian of whom all the whites speak well, he finished by saying*

Bitterroot Salish Chief Charlo (1830–1910) and his family, 1908. *Courtesy Library of Congress.*

> *it was my fathers* [sic] *boast that his hand had never in seventy years been bloodied with the white mans* [sic] *blood. And I am the son of my father. He went on to say that his peoples* [sic] *hearts were the same as his heart and that all would remain friendly.*[96]

Charlo went on to say that he would not fight his friends the Nez Perce, but he would not stop his warriors if some of them wished to help the captain. About a dozen eventually joined the soldiers.

When Rawn had first arrived in Missoula, the people of the Bitterroot had asked him to put scouts on Lolo Pass and throughout the valley. At the time, he lamented that if he had 150 men he could not possibly cover the entire area. He did agree that if a dozen or more horses and saddles were furnished by the settlers, he would put scouts in two of the most dreaded passes. Since the horses were not furnished, he did not post any guards. On July 6, the *Weekly Missoulian* defended this decision:

> *Captain Rawn, commander of the Missoula post, is fully sensible of the gravity of the situation in this locality. He recognizes the importance of having videttes posted along the LoLo and Elk City trails, but he has no horses with his command, and he has not a sufficient force at this disposal to detach for this service and have work proceed at the post. He is in constant communication with his superior officers, and holds himself in readiness to act promptly in case we are menaced with an invasion from the west.*

Now, with the imminent arrival of the Nez Perce, the Bitterroot settlers provided two horses and the necessary equipment. Rawn sent an officer and four soldiers to Lolo Pass with orders to watch for the approach of the Indians.[97] Leaving on July 18, Second Lieutenant Francis Woodbridge and the four enlisted men went up Lolo Canyon to reconnoiter. Receiving no word from them by July 21, Rawn dispatched First Lieutenant Charles Coolidge to proceed to the pass and go as far as he prudently could, furnishing Rawn with any news about Woodbridge and the Nez Perce. On July 22, Lieutenant Coolidge met Lieutenant Woodbridge and party, who were returning to Missoula after scouting the Lolo Trail as far as the Clearwater in Idaho in vain. On that same day, a half-breed who had been a prisoner of the Nez Perce caught up with them and told them that the Nez Perce were coming. Lieutenant Woodbridge dispatched a courier immediately to Captain Rawn, and the news spread such alarm that the citizens of Missoula and the Bitterroot began forming volunteer companies to protect themselves.[98]

On July 25, Rawn wrote to the district adjutant at Fort Shaw that he was entrenching twenty-five regulars, each equipped with four days of rations and one hundred rounds of ammunition. About fifty volunteers had already joined him in Lolo Canyon. While hopeful of more volunteers, he was not counting on them. He asked for more troops and declared his intention to meet with the Nez Perce the next day to inform them that unless they disarmed and dismounted, he would give them a fight. He concluded, "White Bird says he will go through peaceably, if he can, but will go through. This news is entirely reliable."[99]

More volunteers did show up, from the Bitterroot and Missoula. Captain C.P. Higgins rallied the Missoulians to serve under volunteer Captain Kenney; interestingly, Higgins declined to participate personally because his life insurance policy prohibited him.[100] Those volunteering acted for many reasons—some sought to protect their homes, but many, juiced up with whiskey-courage, also volunteered for fun, excitement and the possibility of plunder.

On that same day, Captain Kenney, with four men, met the chiefs near the Nez Perce campsite below Woodman's ranch. He told them that although he had no authority to negotiate, he would arrange for them to meet Captain Rawn.

Arriving in Lolo Canyon later on July 25, Rawn chose what he considered to be the most defensible and least easily flanked part of the canyon about four miles east of the mouth of the canyon and two miles west of the Nez Perce camp. "My intentions were with my force '5 commissioned officers and 30 enlisted men' and assisted by the citizen volunteers, to compel the Indians to surrender their arms and ammunitions and to dispute their passage by force of arms, into the Bitter-root valley."[101] They immediately commenced felling trees and digging their entrenchment and rifle pits as more volunteers arrived, increasing the force to perhaps 200 or 250.

Confident that the people of Montana were peaceful, Looking Glass, White Bird and Joseph went to the barricade under a white flag of truce. The soldiers and volunteers held their fire as, in awe, they watched the great chiefs ride up unafraid, dismount and shake hands with Captain Rawn. Looking at the fortifications, half-built and only two to three logs high, Looking Glass laughingly described them as a corral. The chiefs parlayed with the officers and delegates of the volunteers through the interpreter, Delaware Jim. They were friendly, and it was all very unreal to the soldiers—these were supposed to be hostiles!

A photograph of the Rice or trowel bayonet, invented by General Edmund Rice in 1869. A combination bayonet and hand shovel, or trowel, it could be used on the end of a Springfield rifle as a weapon but was also developed to dig quick field entrenchments such as those at Lolo Canyon and the Battle of the Big Hole. *Courtesy the Historical Museum at Fort Missoula Education Collection.*

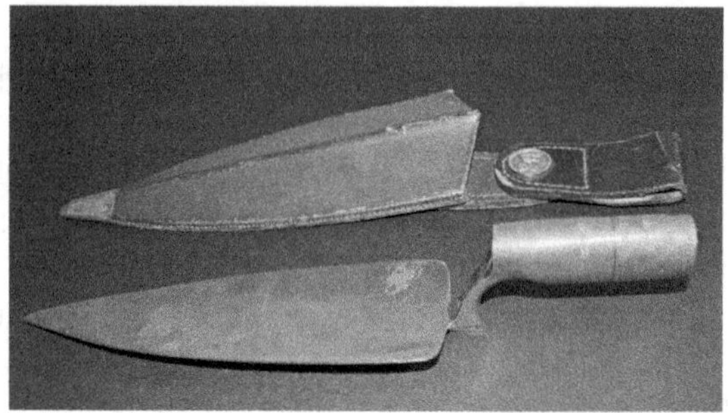

A view looking east from the approximate area where the Nez Perce camped in Lolo Canyon. Captain Rawn and his men were located about two miles to the east. *Author's photograph.*

Looking Glass believed that they had left the war behind in Idaho and did not want to fight their friends in Montana. He promised that if allowed to pass unmolested, the Nez Perce would go up the Bitterroot Valley in peace on their way to the buffalo country in eastern Montana. Rawn replied that he could not let them go unless they surrendered their weapons. White Bird objected, citing the 1858 Indian war in which the whites had persuaded the Palouses, Yakimas, Spokanes and Coeur d'Alenes to surrender their arms and then had them hanged.

On July 26, Governor Benjamin Potts arrived and accompanied Captain Rawn and an escort of fifty to meet the Indians again. The Nez Perce formed a watchful line in case of any war-like move by the soldiers. Looking Glass, Joseph and two others rode forward. The meeting lasted about half an hour while the warriors on both sides anxiously watched. Rawn repeated his demands. Looking Glass requested another meeting for the next day.[102]

On July 27, Rawn reported, apparently misinformed about Chief Charlo's intentions:

> *Had a talk with Joseph and Looking-Glass this afternoon and told them they had to surrender arms and ammunition or fight. They are to consider tonight. I think that for want of ammunition or Charlo's threat they are wavering. Charlo has sent them word, that if they come into the Bitter Root he will fight them. He has already sent me some of his Warriors.*[103]

For the purpose of gaining time for General Howard to fall upon the rear of the Nez Perce and for Colonel Gibbon to arrive from Fort Shaw, Rawn scheduled another meeting for July 28. On that day, he and his interpreter met with Looking Glass and one other Indian. The meeting took place in the open prairie, out of rifle distance of either camp. Rawn submitted the same terms: if they wanted to enter the Bitterroot Valley, they would have to disarm, dismount and surrender all of their stock. Surprisingly or disingenuously, Looking Glass said that he would talk to his people and report back at 9:00 a.m. the next day. Distrusting him, Rawn proposed noon, and they separated without agreement. Rawn reported that he "returned to the breastworks expecting to be attacked."[104]

Reminiscences and accounts differ on much of what happened next, but several accounts say that Looking Glass and the chiefs met to discuss Rawn's ultimatum, with much argument. According to White Bird, Joseph proposed going around the fortifications, passing the soldiers in peace and fighting only if they had to. There were currents of jealousy and distrust of Looking Glass as Looking Glass asserted that the bands had made him their leader and he would get them past the barricades without fighting. Looking Glass's confidence may explain the improbable version that he had made a deal with Rawn that if they moved through the area peacefully, no one would attack them in Montana.[105]

Word reached the volunteers behind the fortifications that the Nez Perce had promised to pass peaceably through their valley if they were allowed to pass the soldiers without engaging in battle; the implied threat was that if

A re-creation of what the entrenchments at Lolo Canyon would have looked like, at the Lolo National Forest Picnic Ground, "Historic Site Fort Fizzle," Department of Agriculture. *Author's photograph.*

they had to fight, they would win, and then they would take their revenge in the valley. That night, Rawn reported "some 100 or more, representing Bitter-root valley, hearing that the Nez-Perces promised to pass peaceably through it, determined that no act of hostility on their part should provoke the Indians to a contrary measure, and without leave left in squads of from one to a dozen."[106]

He then reported the Nez Perces' next move:

> *On the 28th the Indians moved from the canyon to the hills, ascending the sides one half mile in my front, passed my flank and went into the Bitter-root valley. As soon as I found that they were passing around me, and hearing that they had attacked a rear guard I had established to prevent desertions, I abandoned this breastworks, formed a skirmish line across the canyon with my regulars and such of the volunteers as I could control and advanced in the direction the Indians had gone.*
>
> *They did not accept a fight but retreated up the Bitter-root. At the mouth of the Loo Loo and before reaching it, all the volunteers had left me, but a dozen to twenty Missoula men, and I was obliged to return to this post.*[107]

W.R. Logan, son of Captain William Logan, provided one eyewitness account:

> *About ten o'clock we heard singing, apparently above our heads. Upon looking up we discovered the Indians passing along the side of the cliff, where we thought a goat could not pass, much less an entire tribe of Indians with all their impedimenta. The entire band dropped into the valley behind us and then proceeded up the Bitter Root. Two civilians and I rode down from our camp and followed the Indians for a mile or more. They were good-natured, cracked jokes, and seemed very much amused at the way they had fooled Rawn and Logan.*[108]

Yellow Wolf provided another eyewitness account:

> *Early next morning the families packed to move. We found a different way to go by those soldiers. While a few warriors climbed among rocks and fired down on the soldier fort, the rest of the Indians with our horse herds struck to the left of main trail. I could see the soldiers from the mountainside where we traveled. It was no trouble, not dangerous, to pass those soldiers.*[109]

A view looking north from the entrenchments in Lolo Canyon. The Nez Perce escaped the soldiers by going around them over these mountains and then descending back into the valley. *Author's photograph.*

To escape, the warriors created a screen, lining themselves among the trees and rocks on Rawn's northern flank while the chiefs led the families up the gulch about half a mile upstream of the soldiers. At the top, they turned east and proceeded to bypass the entrenchments. Six soldiers and volunteers, detailed earlier that day to climb the mountain and spy on the Indians, saw the Nez Perce start up the gulch and were almost cut off before they could get word to Rawn. The Nez Perce were seen high on the mountain hastening past the barricade toward Sleeman Creek and the valley beyond. Some soldiers or volunteers shot, and the warriors returned fire from their hiding places. Rawn ordered thirty to forty of the remaining volunteers to attack, but by then the Nez Perce had disappeared.

Rawn reorganized his men into a skirmish line across the canyon and led them downstream where he had left a rear guard to prevent more deserters from escaping. On the way downstream, the Flathead Indians and more volunteers left for home. Several miles down the canyon, Rawn could see the Nez Perce ascending the Bitterroot Valley. Not willing to risk a fight with so few soldiers, Rawn halted his men until the last Indian disappeared. By the time Rawn reached the mouth of the canyon, the Nez Perce had had a few brief firefights with his rearguard and an isolated and frightened group of volunteers. The Nez Perce captured three citizens but let them go, admonishing them to return home and tell everyone that the Nez Perce would not bother the settlers.

Outmaneuvered and outnumbered, with a small group of regular soldiers and perhaps twenty Missoula volunteers, Rawn went back to Missoula to wait for Howard or Gibbon.[110]

Rawn soon became the subject of much criticism and jokes, as the "battle" was laughingly referred to as "Fort Fizzle." Worse than that, he was accused of drunkenness. In 1969, volunteer M.M. McCauley's grandson told a highly implausible family tale that "it was decided by the volunteers that it would be a disastrous venture to try to fight. They knew Captain Rawn could not resist whiskey and sent out for enough to put him under until the Indians passed by." Volunteer Wilson B. Harlan maintained that Rawn and Logan were both drunk to the point of being passed out. This seems highly unlikely, and one has to take into consideration any statement made by a deserter about his superior, particularly since Rawn had called the volunteers out as deserters and had not only established a rear guard to stop them but also had ordered his lieutenants to forcibly stop them.

It is true that alcohol was used greatly by the officers and men of the military, Rawn included. As early as March 1863, records indicate that

Rawn placed a very large order for alcohol while a lieutenant at Fort Union, New Mexico; but it must be noted that by March 1863, the New Mexican region was a very inactive area, and it is also possible that Rawn was purchasing supplies for other officers as well.[111] It is also true that Rawn was still suffering from his foot and leg injury of 1873. In fact, that condition plagued him to the extent that he would be on leave from October 1878 through May 1879, appearing before an Army Retiring Board in New York City at the end of March and early April of that year to see if the injury warranted his retirement from the army. Ultimately, the board decided that the injury did not incapacitate enough him for service, but he was obviously still suffering.[112] With alcohol the main self-medication on the frontier, it is not surprising that Rawn used it. There are many receipts in the personal collection of historian Kermit Edmunds, of Missoula, signed by Rawn for alcohol, as there are in some of the research files that are available. However, unlike in the case of Major Baker, there is no official record of his drinking, nor were any of his actions criticized by any of his superiors.

Perhaps an explanation for the presence of whiskey in Lolo Canyon is found in the *Weekly Missoulian* of July 20, when it wrote that "Captain Rawn, while out hunting last week, was thrown from his horse while in the act of discharging his piece, and received injuries to his spine which will confine him to his bed for some time." If there was whiskey present, again, one suspects it was of a medicinal nature.

At issue, more than any use of alcohol, was simply the fact that Rawn had allowed the Nez Perce to escape. Despite initial criticism, Chauncey Barbour, editor of the Missoula paper, came to support Rawn's decision. The *Weekly Missoulian* for July 27 quoted Governor Potts as saying, "It would be madness for us to attack the Nez Perces with our inadequate force." In that same edition, the editor wrote, "Capt. Rawn was censured without stint Saturday night; but, as an intelligent view of the whole situation discloses itself, we are fully prepared to say that he pursued a course of wisdom and showed an intelligent care for the best welfare of the people of Missoula county." And "to allow the Indians to pass by without a blow may have been disgraceful; to attack them with 250 raw and inexperienced men would have been madness and folly."

If one looks at *The Army Officer's Pocket Companion*, Article 67, Order of Battle, Rawn's course of action is vindicated. The *Pocket Companion* states that it is necessary to "avoid a battle if you think the consequences of a defeat would be more serious than the advantages to be expected from a victory; if the enemy occupies an impregnable position; if you have not all your troop;

and if you hope that in time, fatigue, sickness, scarcity, or discord will do your work."

To clear his name, after his return from the Battle of the Big Hole, Rawn requested a court-martial or court of inquiry. Colonel Gibbon closed the case as he directed his adjutant to return the request, stating, "It is the opinion of the District Commander that no such vindication of Captain Rawn as asked for is required. If the Battle of the Big Hole does not vindicate us all from previous aspersions of irresponsible newspapers it is not thought a Court can do it."[113]

More succinctly, in describing what happened in Lolo Canyon, Sergeant Charles Loynes stated that they were under the command of Captain Charles C. Rawn, "and a better officer never lived."[114]

CHAPTER 9

# THE BATTLE OF THE BIG HOLE

After bypassing the $7^{th}$ Infantry in Lolo Canyon, the Nez Perce proceeded peacefully up the Bitterroot Valley, trading with the settlers and businessmen of the area while some white families, not trusting the peaceful intentions of the Indians, sought protection in old Fort Owen. There were only two minor disturbances during the Indians' journey up the valley. In one instance, a merchant violated an agreement not to serve alcohol to an Indian, and when a warrior became drunk, Looking Glass had him seized and sent to camp under guard. A second instance occurred when some young warriors discovered and ransacked the deserted cabin of Myron Lockwood, making away with some supplies. Upon their return to camp, Looking Glass made them leave three of their horses in Lockwood's field after first branding them with Lockwood's brand. Throughout most of the Indians' passage, the white citizens were mainly curious, while the Nez Perce were generally amused by the attitude of the whites. At a hastily constructed fort near Skalkaho, the Nez Perces' friendliness and amusement reassured the settlers so much that it was reported they even sold bullets to the Indians.

On their passage through the area, the Nez Perce were joined by some other Nez Perce who lived in the valley. This included a footloose half-French, half-Nez Perce warrior named Lean Elk, known to the white men as Poker Joe for his love of the game. Lean Elk had been on his way across the Lolo Trail on a visit to Idaho when he hurt himself hunting. When stopped by some white men, he tried to explain what had happened. They refused to believe him, thought he had been injured in the Idaho battles and threatened to detain him. Angered by this, he joined the warring Nez Perce as they came through. He was a welcome addition, not only for his knowledge of the area but also for his leadership abilities, which the Indians would later rely on.

Captain Charles C. Rawn, circa 1877. *Courtesy National Park Service, Big Hole National Battlefield.*

While the Nez Perce made their way slowly, and peacefully, up the valley, Captain Rawn returned to his new fort in Missoula but also sent two volunteer scouts, John Deschamps and Bob Irvine, to follow the Indians to determine where they were headed. Although their intention to go to the buffalo country in eastern Montana was known, it was still possible that from the top of the Bitterroot Valley, at Lost Trail Pass, they could turn back west to their traditional homeland in Idaho.

True to his word, Looking Glass led the Nez Perce east into the Big Hole River Basin and made camp at the junction of Trail and Ruby Creeks, just below the slope of the mountains, an area used for centuries by Salish and Nez Perce hunting parities on their way to and from the plains. This area was called by its Salish name, *Izhkumzzizlakik Pah*, place of the picket pin, pot gut or sage rat, an animal smaller than a ground squirrel. The Nez Perce pastured their pony herd of almost two thousand part of the way up the mountain. On August 7, their first day of rest in weeks, the Indians commenced working, recovered from their travails and enjoyed themselves. However, several of the chiefs and warriors were uneasy at the slow pace maintained by Looking Glass and at his failure to post guards around the camp. When White Bird and others attempted to force Looking Glass to post sentries, he adamantly refused and forbade them to post their own. Looking Glass was confident that they had left the war and General Howard far behind in Idaho, and he did not want to give the whites an excuse to make war with them in Montana. Besides, he told them they needed time to rest, it was calm and they would stay the next day. They spent the next day cutting and peeling lodge poles to replace the tipi poles they had lost in Idaho. Some of the men hunted, but most relaxed around camp and played the stick and bone game. The women dug camas roots, and the children played.[115]

Not all were so sanguine; the warrior Wahlitits told of a dream he had: "My brothers, my sisters, I am telling you! In a dream last night I saw myself killed. I will be killed soon! I do not care. I am willing to die. But first, I will kill some soldiers. I shall not turn back from the death. We are all going to die!"[116] Lone Bird, another great warrior, proclaimed, "My shaking heart tells me trouble and death will overtake us if we make no hurry through this land! I can not smother, I can not hide that which I see. I must speak what is revealed to me. Let us begone to the buffalo country!"[117] Others also had dreams or visions. Looking Glass paid no attention.

While the Indians moved slowly up the Bitterroot Valley, Colonel Gibbon prepared to march south from Fort Shaw to battle the Nez Perce. At the same time, he called on Governor Potts to raise a volunteer force of 300 to prevent the Nez Perce from leaving the Bitterroot. The army denied the governor's authority to pay the militia, and the volunteers from Butte and Deer Lodge were quickly, though temporarily, disbanded. Meanwhile, Gibbon had already ordered Captain George Browning and Company G from Fort Ellis to support Captain Rawn in Missoula. They arrived on July 30, after a forced march of 240 miles. At Fort Shaw, Gibbon assembled Companies D, F and K and marched toward Missoula, bringing a mountain howitzer with him. On August 3, he arrived at Fort Missoula, where he picked up Captain Rawn's and Captain Logan's two companies and Captain Browning's company. On August 4, leaving about a dozen soldiers behind to continue to build the new fort and protect his rear, Gibbon, along with 15 officers and 146 men, followed the Nez Perce up the Bitterroot at a quick pace. Along the way, they picked up about 75 volunteers, about half of whom turned back before reaching the pass to the Big Hole Valley. Gibbon's force numbered 182 as they crossed the Continental Divide. Sergeant Loynes reported that they "followed over the roughest country imaginable. In places the trail was so steep that the mules were detached from the Army wagons and with ropes were drawn up the steep sides."[118]

Lieutenant James Bradley took a scouting detail ahead of the main body of soldiers, hoping to find the Nez Perce camp and drive off their pony herd in advance of Gibbon's arrival. Although he found the camp, it was too far away, and he had to wait for the main force. Bradley and his scouts may have been the gray figures that some of the Indians later recalled seeing that night.

Abandoning his supply wagons, Gibbon sped forward to meet up with Bradley's scouts, finding them five miles from the Nez Perce camp just before sunset on August 8. They stopped to rest and wait for the wagons to catch up. At 11:00 p.m., Gibbon ordered his men to divest themselves of all they would not need for a quick battle—jackets, blanket rolls, etc.—taking with them only their rifles, one hundred rounds of ammunition each and a few canteens. All animals except Gibbon's and few other officers' horses were left behind. They proceeded east, along the trail discovered by Lieutenant Bradley. Now numbering 149 soldiers and 35 civilian volunteers, they marched in silence through the cool, clear night. Soon they saw the campfires of the Indian village of eighty-nine tipis in the distance across the river. The soldiers stealthily crept ahead. The Indians' horses gently neighed and a few dogs barked, but the Indian camp remained quiet. For two hours, the soldiers lay in ambush positions, waiting for dawn to break.

First Lieutenant James H. Bradley (1844–1877), 7th Infantry, who died in the first minutes of the Battle of the Big Hole, August 9, 1877; no date. *Courtesy the Montana Historical Society Research Center, Montana Historical Society, Helena, Montana.*

Gibbon had achieved what few officers ever could in the Indian Wars: the element of total surprise. Outnumbered, the best way to use that advantage was to launch a devastating attack, firing low into the tipis, driving the Indians out of their camp and separating them from their animals. While of questionable modern morality, this plan of attack was designed to cut short a potentially lengthy war; if innocents were killed, it was a price the army was willing to pay. Besides, if the army had learned anything, it was that Indian battles were fought where no quarter was asked for, and none given, by either side.

At 4:00 a.m. on August 9, the men crept forward through the dense willows along the riverside. Although the exact disposition of some of the companies is not clear in the records, Bradley led on the left with his volunteers and some soldiers, Captain James Sanno's K Company was in the middle and Captain Richard Comba's D Company took the right flank.

Following closely were Captain Browning's Company G, Captain Logan's A Company, Captain Constant Williams's F Company and Company I under Captain Rawn, some of whom remained in temporary reserve. Fifty yards ahead of them lay the Nez Perce.

As the men pressed forward, an elderly, half-blind Indian approached on horseback on his way to check the horses. Natalekin did not see the soldiers until he was almost upon them, and several volunteers shot him before he could ride off to warn the camp. Although Natalekin lay dead, the shots had awakened the sleeping Nez Perce. Hearing the shots, the 7th Infantry immediately stood up, started firing into the village and charged forward. Lieutenant Bradley was killed by the first Indian response, and the men under his command were left leaderless and ineffective. The soldiers tried to set fire to the tipis but in the early morning dew only produced smoke and more confusion. Within minutes, the reserve companies were called upon to join the fray. Sergeant Loynes wrote:

> *We had previously received orders to give three volleys through the camp and then charge, so that as the Indians stepped up the bank on our side of the stream, they instantly fell, and as we gave three volleys into the camp we rushed to the water's edge, everyone seeming to want to get to the opposite side first. So into the water we leaped, not knowing its depth in the dim light of the moon,* [waded] *through it and into the camp of the Indians. We followed with a yell that would do credit to the Indians themselves.*
>
> *We will never forget that day, how we fought with those savages, kill or be killed, no time to load our rifles. With the butts and muzzles of our guns we struck right and left. The shouts of soldiers, the war whoops of the Indians, the screeching of the squaws, who with Winchesters in their hands were as much to be feared as the bucks. Our attack was a complete surprise, and we gradually forced them back to the opposite side of their camp, where the river makes a complete bend. Into the water they jumped, some of them who had a blanket first throwing it in and getting underneath, trying thus to escape. But they had to have air, so as soon as we discovered this trick we only had to notice where the blanket or buffalo hide was slightly raised, and a bullet at that spot would be sufficient for the body to float down the stream. Although at this time the sun had not yet risen, it was quite light.*[119]

Panic ensued in the village with screams and shouts as bullets ripped through tipis and smoke whirled around. Some warriors were too dazed to react immediately. Women grabbed their children and unwittingly ran right into the soldiers' fire. Soldiers waded through the river and charged at the tipis, firing and clubbing everything that moved. But the Nez Perce soon recovered and began fighting back under the leadership of White Bird, Ollokot, Lean Elk, Looking Glass and others. Joseph did not have a gun and shielded his new baby with his body at the beginning of the battle before leading the horses away from danger. Later, with the troopers pinned down, Joseph brought the horses back as he carried out his responsibilities as the guardian of the families. Because Gibbon did not have enough men to outflank the entire village, many Indians escaped to the south and began to fire back at the soldiers from the brush.

Inside the camp, chaos reigned. Most of the soldiers probably had no desire to kill women or children, but it happened. The men fired wildly, indiscriminately, at anything that moved, as shots came back at them from every direction. A young boy or woman picking up a discarded rifle was to be feared as much as a warrior. Captain Logan was involved in some of the fiercest hand-to-hand fighting in the village, and just as he killed a young warrior (perhaps Wahlitits), the warrior's sister or wife picked up a gun and shot the captain between the eyes. (After Logan's death, Camp Baker was renamed Fort Logan, and the small town of Logan, Montana, was also named after him. And while there was little mutilation of the soldiers, apparently Captain Logan's ring fingers were cut off so that the Indians could get his two rings: a Masonic ring and a signet ring from Scotland that had been in his family for generations. Incredibly, these rings were returned to his family when a friend recognized the signet ring on the finger of a trapper. In 1900, Logan's son recognized the Masonic ring on the finger of a Blackfeet woman, purchased it and returned it to his mother twenty-three years after the captain's death.)

Battle at such close quarters gave little time for thought or circumspection. Yet at times the soldiers displayed compassion, as when one officer ordered his men not to fire on a group of women cowering in the river.

The battle in the village lasted for only twenty minutes before it became obvious to Colonel Gibbon, who suffered a serious leg wound crossing the river, that they had to retreat. He ordered Rawn to screen the withdrawal, and Rawn's men continued to fight at close quarters with the Indians as they slowly withdrew to the west toward a small outcropping, or bench, or point of timber about four hundred yards away. As they retreated, the soldiers could only watch as the Nez Perce killed their wounded brethren left behind. Sergeant Loynes recalled:

*Left*: Captain William Logan (1832–1877), 7th Infantry, who died in hand-to-hand combat in the center of the Nez Perce camp at the Battle of the Big Hole, August 9, 1877; no date. *Courtesy the Montana Historical Society Research Center, Montana Historical Society, Helena, Montana.*

*Below*: A view of the bench of timber where the soldiers of the 7th Infantry took cover after the Nez Perce drove them from the village. There were many more trees in 1877, but the mountain pine beetle has been killing millions of pine trees in the West since the current outbreak. *Author's photograph.*

> *Among the last to leave the camp was Captain Rawn and the few members of his company. Recrossing the creek* [and] *going in a westerly direction for about two hundred and fifty yards, they met the main body trying to entrench by throwing up the dirt using the Rice trowel bayonet for the purpose. One man would scrape up the dirt, while every second man would continue to fire. We were now completely surrounded by the savages, some of whom would climb the trees on the upper side of us. But our best marksmen soon dislodged them. We now lay in a square, probably forty feet each way, the Indians on every side, and not a man expecting to leave alive.*[120]

The soldiers forced the few warriors out of the timber and began to hastily dig rifle pits with their trowel bayonets, hands, spoons and knives as the Indians soon had the entire force surrounded. The Nez Perce fired on the soldiers from every direction, picking off anyone accidentally showing himself, including Lieutenant William English of Rawn's company, who was hit in the back, the bullet lodging in his abdomen.

As the soldiers dug in, Gibbon's howitzer appeared on the mountain to their west. The untrained crew managed to get off two shots to no effect before the Indians attacked, killed Corporal Sale, wounded two sergeants and sent the rest running. Peopeo Tholekt wanted to use the howitzer against the soldiers, but the Indians could not operate the cannon, so they dismantled it and buried the barrel. Later, Lean Elk rolled it over a bluff into the brush. Meanwhile, they made off with the two thousand rounds of small arms ammunition it carried.

The Nez Perce tried to set the grass on fire to drive the soldiers into the open, but the grass was too wet and the soldiers were saved. Another time, the warrior Five Wounds charged on foot at the soldiers and was immediately killed. His best friend, Rainbow, had been killed earlier that day, and they had promised each other that they would die on the same

Location of Colonel Gibbon's mountain howitzer, with the Big Hole Valley beyond. *Author's photograph.*

A replica of the original mountain howitzer that managed to get off two shots before being captured and destroyed by the Nez Perce. *Author's photograph.*

day just as their fathers had done; both Five Wounds and Rainbow had been supporters of Looking Glass.

The Nez Perce positioned themselves to keep the soldiers pinned down while the rest of the tribe escaped. The village was a scene of mournful wailing and tears as thirty lay dead in camp. Twenty were dead or dying alongside the river, and more lay on the opposite side. Hahtalekin, the Palus leader, was dead. Wahlitits was dead. The beloved war leader Rainbow was dead. Joseph's wife was wounded, as was Ollokot's wife. Now the Nez Perce knew that they were not safe from the army in Montana and it was time to run again, quickly. While Joseph supervised the preparations for leaving, the warriors kept the soldiers occupied. The grieving survivors quickly made up their packs, took down a few tipis, hastily buried their dead in a common grave under the riverbank and built travois to carry the wounded.

The soldiers spent the rest of the day and the entire night besieged and pinned down. They were parched for lack of water and because of the inhalation of smoke throughout the day until Privates Coon, Hines and Welsh volunteered to take some canteens down to the river, perhaps thirty yards below them. Their compatriots poured volley after volley into the bushes ahead of them to drive off any Indians, and miraculously, the

A view looking east from the mountain howitzer's location, past the bench of timber where the soldiers were surrounded to the location of the Nez Perce camp in the center of the photograph. *Author's photograph.*

volunteers filled the canteens and got back to their lines with the much-needed water.

The soldiers were also cold. They had left their jackets and blankets at the previous night's camp, and after fighting all day through the water and heat, the temperature now dropped and they could not risk starting any fires. They had also not eaten since the night before, and any of the hardtack that they brought along had dissolved in their pockets as they fought through the river. In desperation, some carved off and ate the meat of Lieutenant Woodruff's dead, bloated horse.

Beyond the physical trials, the emotional toll was tremendous. Throughout the long night, the cries and moans of the wounded were intense, and the bullets kept coming at them. They were also scared; had the Nez Perce wanted to massacre them, it would have been another Custer's battlefield.

The night and the nightmare dragged on.

At dawn on August 10, Nelse McGilliam, a civilian courier from General Howard, arrived. Howard was still a day away, but the Nez Perce were now aware that he was coming, so they fired a few parting shots over the soldiers and followed the rest of their camp fleeing to the south. Gibbon sent Captain Browning and a patrol back to bring the supply wagons forward.

August 10 was quiet in camp. Gibbon did not have a surgeon; First Lieutenant Charles Coolidge acted in that capacity, but he was severely injured with a shot through both legs, a crippling wound to one hand and a third wound in one heel that prevented him from doing much. Lieutenant Woodruff stepped in and did what he could, using tobacco juice to cleanse the wounds and gunpowder and a match to cauterize them. In reality, the maggots that quickly appeared were the best medicine, as they helped clean the wounds.

The men of the 7th Infantry had suffered greatly. Three officers were killed and four wounded; twenty-two enlisted men were killed and twenty-nine wounded. The volunteers suffered six killed and four wounded. It is estimated that between sixty and ninety Nez Perce were killed, about two-thirds of them women and children.

The next day, General Howard and his advance party arrived.

Captain Comba was placed in charge of the burial party, a difficult job since Captain Logan was his father-in-law. Gibbon placed Captain Rawn in charge of the hospital train, which slowly limped the ninety-five miles to Deer Lodge, where Montana's first surgical hospital—St. Joseph's Hospital, run by the Sisters of Charity—was located. Among the wounded was the mortally injured Lieutenant English.

During the battle, Gibbon had sent a messenger, Billie Edwards, to Deer Lodge for help. William A. Clark, banker and future Copper King, had taken charge, reassembled the volunteers in Butte and collected wagons and supplies. When the volunteer contingents from Butte, Deer Lodge, Philipsburg, Beartown, Pioneer City, Silver Bow, Flint Creek, Granite, Henderson Gulch, Georgetown and Helena joined in the Big Hole Valley, they had five surgeons, twenty-eight light wagons and ambulances and two companies of volunteers. When this relief column was within thirteen miles of the battlefield, a messenger from Gibbon asked them to wait. When the 7th Infantry arrived, the surgeons redressed the wounds and did everything possible to make the soldiers comfortable. Here Gibbon left for Deer Lodge in a buggy and left Rawn in command. The battered soldiers reached town on August 16 and received excellent care from the people of the area. On the last day before arriving in Deer Lodge, Lieutenant English's wife of a few months, Kate, arrived from Missoula. Though aware of his condition, she did her best to cheer her husband and the rest of the soldiers. Unfortunately, the wound was fatal, and the lieutenant died on August 20. He was given a Masonic burial with military honors; it was the finest funeral seen in

Montana to that time. His body was later moved to Jacksonville, Indiana. Kate never remarried.

While the seriously wounded remained in the hospital in Deer Lodge, the rest reported to their respective posts as Gibbon disbanded his force. Captain Rawn, with Companies A, D, G and I, returned to Missoula on August 21 to continue constructing the new fort.[121]

Reporting on the battle on August 17, the *Weekly Missoulian* wrote, "The gallant officers of the Seventh Regiment infused a spirit of heroism into every man on the battle field at the Big Hole, and made it one of the most memorable battles of modern times." It went on to quote Sam Dunham, a compositor for the paper who was at the battle: "Capt. Rawn is deserving of especial mention for his bravery and coolness in the presence of appalling danger. After his chief was wounded the direction of affairs largely devolved on him, and it was grand to witness the readiness in which the men followed where he went and their confidence in his leadership."

Captain Rawn and the 7th Infantry remained at Fort Missoula until August 14, 1877, when they were replaced by Lieutenant Colonel John Brooke and four companies of the 3rd Infantry. Until then, they continued to work on constructing fort buildings and engaged in some mop-up operations with the Nez Perce, as the fort served as a jail for several Indians captured in the area. The Post Council of Administration convened and recommended to the secretary of war that Captain Logan's son and his partner, Theodore Shed, be engaged as the post traders.[122] Acting on information that several of the graves had been opened and that bodies had been dragged to the surface by bears and other animals, on September 20, Rawn sent a detachment consisting of Second Lieutenant John Van Orsdale and six enlisted men to go to the battlefield to reinter the bodies of their comrades who had fallen in that battle.[123]

All returned to routine as they recovered from the ravages of the battle, as General Howard continued his pursuit of the fleeing Nez Perce.

CHAPTER *10*

# THE NEZ PERCE, PART II

After allowing the Nez Perce time to get a head start of one hundred miles, General Howard finally began his pursuit on August 13, the day Gibbon and the shattered 7th Infantry started for Deer Lodge.

Meanwhile, with so many dead, Looking Glass was no longer trusted, and the Nez Perce turned to Lean Elk, who knew the Montana trails and the route to where Sitting Bull was in Canada.[124] Under Lean Elk's leadership, the Nez Perce briefly turned west, crossed the Continental Divide and temporarily descended back into Idaho. No longer as trusting or as peaceful as they had been in the Bitterroot Valley, some warriors killed some settlers and stole horses on Horse Prairie Creek, Montana, on August 12 and attacked a freight wagon train and killed more whites on Birch Creek, in Idaho, on August 15.

Howard's treaty Nez Perce guides told him that the hostile bands were following a traditional route that would take them into Yellowstone National Park. Howard initially seized the opportunity to intercept them by taking a shorter route but in the end was talked out of it by volunteers and by his desire to protect a stagecoach line to the south. Still a day behind, Howard stopped at Camas Meadows on August 19 and camped on the same grounds the Indians had abandoned that morning. During the night, about 225 Nez Perce warriors, under the tactical command of Looking Glass, returned to steal Howard's livestock, needing the animals to replace those they had lost and to trade with settlers. A lively skirmish ensued, and the Nez Perce made off with 150 army mules. Howard's

*The Nez Perce War*, from sketches of an army officer, 1877. *Courtesy Library of Congress.*

cavalry gave chase and eventually recovered some of the mules before retreating from a bitter counterattack by the Indians.

The Nez Perce had escaped, again.

Acting with unusual foresight, Howard sent forces to block Targhee Pass into Yellowstone National Park to hold the Indians while he fell on their rear. Unfortunately, after waiting a short time, Lieutenant Bacon decided that the Nez Perce had taken a different route and left; the Nez Perce crossed the pass three days later. Ahead of them were eight or nine parties of tourists, totaling at least thirty-five. Notably, one party of tourists that included General Sherman had departed the park only days earlier. Inside the park, the Nez Perce terrorized and killed several tourists and miners and attacked and robbed stores at Mammoth Falls. Meanwhile, Howard's forces rested by Henry's Lake as the general and a few aides traveled to Virginia City to obtain supplies and telegraph Generals Sherman and Sheridan.

In response to Howard's request to return to Idaho and let the army troops in eastern Montana deal with the Nez Perce, General Sheridan bluntly informed the general that it was still his job, and on August 28, Howard resumed his pursuit. The day before, Colonel Gibbon, still following the progress of the Nez Perce, had sent a cable to General Howard in Virginia City advising him to communicate, through Fort Ellis, with Colonel Samuel Sturgis, of Colonel Miles's command. At the same time, Gibbon received word from Captain Rawn in Missoula that some Spokane Indians were on their way east, presumably to hunt. Gibbon telegraphed Rawn to keep the Spokanes from coming east of Missoula for their own safety because they might be mistaken for the hostile Nez Perce.

General Sherman, uneasy at Howard's progress, decided to send forces from the east to help him. Colonel Sturgis, with a detachment of six troops (companies), was ordered to the mouth of the Clark Fork of the Yellowstone River canyon, near Heart Mountain. While waiting for Colonel Wesley Merritt's 5th Cavalry to take position at the other end of the canyon, Sturgis had to defend both ends. On September 8, a patrol spotted the Nez Perce moving south, and Sturgis moved to cut them off. However, the Nez Perce had already discovered the cavalry blocking their escape route. They feigned to the south to deceive Sturgis, doubled back to the Clark Fork and gained the plains ahead of Sturgis.

Humiliated, Sturgis met with Howard, who allowed him to make a forced march to attempt to catch the Indians. As Sturgis set off, the Nez Perce were slowing down as parties of warriors were raiding settlements in the area and killing a few more whites. On September 13, after raiding the town of Coulson (now Billings), Sturgis's column prepared to attack. The Indians ascended Canyon Creek on the north side of the Yellowstone River and then fell back and fought off the cavalry attacks as their families fled once again. Sturgis tried several tactics, all of which failed, and the Nez Perce escaped again.

Once in Crow territory, the Nez Perce quickly found that the Crow were unwilling to help them, and the Nez Perce made the decision to head north and cross the Great Medicine Line into Canada, where the army could not pursue. The Crow, who had fought the Dakota Sioux with the Nez Perce in 1874, were afraid of the army's retaliation if they helped their former allies. They not only refused to help their friends but also assisted the army by stealing animals from the Nez Perce and passing along information to the army.

As his command continued to chase the Nez Perce, Howard sent a dispatch to Colonel Miles at the Tongue River Cantonment to ask his assistance in stopping the Indians before they could reach Canada. The ever-ambitious Miles, hoping to earn his general's star, needed no further encouragement. Miles received Howard's dispatch on September 17, and by daybreak the next morning, his entire force of five infantry companies and two troops of cavalry were on the move. Moving to the northwest, Mile absorbed four more cavalry troops who were under orders to escort General Terry to Canada to confer with Sitting Bull. Miles now had almost four hundred men, a Hotchkiss gun (a light mountain gun) and a supply train of forty wagons.

At the mouth of the Musselshell River, Miles received word that the Nez Perce had crossed the Missouri River at Cow Island, where they had attacked a lightly held army supply depot on September 23. This depot, used only a short time each year, was made of tents inside earthwork entrenchments. The Nez Perce set up camp nearby, and several warriors went to the depot to buy some food. They received a miserly side of bacon and a bag of hardtack. Later that evening the warriors returned and began firing on the depot and charged three times. Two of the civilian clerks were wounded as the Nez Perce took food and cooking utensils from the stored freight. Sergeant Molchert believed that the only thing that saved them from being totally overrun was that the Indians had set fire to a large tent filled with bacon, and the fire lit up the area so the warriors could not attack without being seen and shot. The Indians continued firing until ten o'clock the next morning, when it was obvious that as long as the soldiers and clerks stayed behind their entrenchments, it was a waste of ammunition to continue firing.

Crossing the Missouri River, the Nez Perce left the last physical barrier to Canada behind them and slowed down. The pace that Lean Elk had set since the Big Hole had been exhausting. They had outfought and outmaneuvered Howard, Gibbon and Sturgis. Looking Glass argued that they had left the army far in the rear and needed rest. Howard encouraged this misconception by deliberately slowing down his pursuit to give Miles a chance to get ahead of the Indians. For five days, the Nez Perce halted early each afternoon, to the great annoyance of Lean Elk, until on September 29, they halted on the northern flank of the Bear Paw Mountains, along Snake Creek, about forty miles south of the Canadian border. The abundant fish and game made this a good place to stop before the final push.

Colonel Nelson Miles (1839–1925), commander of the 5th Infantry at the Tongue River Cantonment, later renamed Fort Keogh, 1876. He was named commanding general of the United States in 1895 and commanded all US forces during the Spanish-American War; he retired in 1903 as a lieutenant general. *Courtesy the Montana Historical Society Research Center, Montana Historical Society, Helena, Montana.*

On September 30, Miles's force intercepted the Nez Perce trail and turned north. About midmorning, the few tipis that had survived the Big Hole Battle came into view, and Miles ordered his cavalry to attack. One cavalry troop made for the pony herd pastured on the land west of the camp. The other unit charged the camp and ran into the staunch defense of the Nez Perce, who had been alerted by the sound of the cavalry's charge at a distance. While those Nez Perce outside the perimeter of the battle either tried to return to camp or started the long trek to Canada on their own, the warriors from the village quickly took a strong defensive position in the old streambanks, deep coulees, rocks and brush surrounding their camp. At a range of two hundred yards, the warriors opened on the charging troopers, who faltered, dismounted and barely hung on until the infantry arrived to help occupy the crest. Yellow Wolf recalled:

Drawing of the Bear Paw Battle from *Harper's* or *Leslie's Weekly*, 1877. *Courtesy the Montana Historical Society Research Center, Montana Historical Society, Helena, Montana.*

> *You have seen hail, sometimes, leveling the grass. Indians were so leveled by the bullet hail. Most of our few warriors left from the Big Hole had been swept as leaves before the storm. Chief Ollokot, Lone Bird, and Lean Elk were gone.*
>
> *Outside the camp I had seen men killed. Soldiers ten, Indians ten. That was not so bad. But now, when I saw our remaining warriors gone, my heart grew choked and heavy.*[125]

After scattering the horses, the army turned to the fleeing Nez Perce and those defending the north end of the camp. At an outcropping of red rocks, Toohoolhoolzote and 5 warriors were killed. Ollokot was killed in a rifle pit on the crest of the ridge nearby. Lean Elk, mistaken for one of Miles's Cheyenne or Crow scouts in the cold drizzle, was killed by his own men. The Nez Perce, about 450 of them, retreated to the north end of camp and dug in with their camas hooks and knives.

Wisely, although reluctantly, Miles halted the attack and placed the Nez Perce camp under siege. Well protected, the Indians easily held off the soldiers, but their horses were gone, their supplies were limited and Miles's Hotchkiss gun began its deadly shelling. Many of their great warrior chiefs were dead, and an early winter storm dropped five inches of snow on the battlefield. There was little hope.

A view of the Bear Paw Battlefield, looking south from the site where Ollokot was killed. *Author's photograph.*

A view of the red rock outcrop where Toohoolhoolzote and five warriors were killed defending the Nez Perce village. *Author's photograph.*

Overview of the Bear Paw Battlefield from one of the Nez Perce rifle pits looking south to the Bear Paw Mountains. *Author's photograph.*

On October 1, Miles displayed a white flag to talk with the remaining chiefs. Looking Glass and White Bird wanted no part of a surrender, hoping to fight their way to Canada. Joseph went to talk with Colonel Miles, but when the talks became unproductive, Miles had Joseph arrested, a direct violation of his own truce flag. However, at the same time a young lieutenant, thinking that the Indians were surrendering, wandered into their lines and was captured. Both sides released their prisoners the next day.

From October 1 to 5, the siege continued. Miles's Civil War mentor, General Howard, arrived on October 4 and generously allowed Miles to remain in command until the Indians surrendered; this would lead to years of bitter argument between the supporters of Miles and Howard. On October 5, the chiefs held council. Joseph was in favor of opening talks with Howard and Miles; Looking Glass and White Bird still wanted to try to fight their way to Canada. Upon leaving the council, Looking Glass was struck by a stray bullet and killed instantly. Joseph then met with Howard and Miles, who promised him that if the Nez Perce surrendered, they would spend the winter at Miles's post on the Yellowstone River and then be returned to the Lapwai Reservation in the spring.

That afternoon, Joseph surrendered his rifle to Miles. First Lieutenant Charles Erskine Scott Wood, aide-de-camp to General Howard, was present and recorded Joseph's words:

> *Tell General Howard I know his heart. What he told me before—I have it in my heart. I am tired of fighting. Too-hul-hul-sit is dead. Looking Glass is dead. He-who-led-the-young-men-in-battle is dead. The chiefs are all dead. It is the young men now who say "yes" or "no." My little daughter has run away upon the prairie. I do not know where to find her—perhaps I shall find her too among the dead. It is cold and we have no fire; no blankets. Our little children are crying for food but we have none to give. Hear me, my chiefs. From where the sun now stands, Joseph will fight no more forever.*[126]

White Bird did not surrender with Joseph, and during the night, he and all but six of his band escaped. When Howard and Miles learned about this escape, they were livid at the apparent breach of promise made by Joseph; they still did not comprehend the nature of tribal leadership. Because of this betrayal, they justified reneging on their promise to Joseph to return the

A view of the site where Chief Joseph surrendered to Colonel Miles and General Howard. *Author's photograph.*

Nez Perce to the reservation. Additionally, General Sherman and General Sheridan did not want the Nez Perce sent back to the reservation, fearing more trouble in Idaho. It was felt that the Nez Perce had to be punished as an example to any other Indian tribe contemplating resistance.

With many Nez Perce still in the area—those who had been outside camp when the battle commenced and those who had managed to escape—Miles and Howard sent some of their troops to search for them. Encouragement was also given to other tribes to round up any of these wandering Nez Perce Indians. The Assiniboine and Gros Ventre eagerly went out of their way to hunt and kill the refugees.

In November, over Miles's protests, the captured Nez Perce (numbering 431, as reported by the War Department) were shipped down the Missouri River from the Tongue River Cantonment to Fort Abraham Lincoln and then by railroad to Fort Leavenworth, Kansas, where they were held as prisoners of war until the Indian Bureau took over. They stayed on a small reserve in Kansas the next spring before they were sent to the Quaker-run Quapaw Agency in the Indian Territory, where the oppressive heat, floods and disease killed dozens. They were transferred then to the Presbyterian Oakland Agency, where they gradually adjusted to the agrarian life, but even here, dysentery, pulmonary diseases and tuberculosis claimed many more as they attempted to acclimate to the harsh new environment.

Joseph never gave up hope of returning to his homeland. With the aid of Miles and many others, including President Garfield's widow, the government finally relented. Joseph and his band of 150 were sent back to the Northwest in 1885—not to Idaho, where Joseph was still held responsible for the murders that started the war, but to the Colville Reservation in Washington. The remaining 118 of Looking Glass's and White Bird's bands were sent to the Lapwai Reservation.

With the help of Howard, Miles and others, the prospect of Joseph returning to his beloved homeland seemed encouraging for a while, but the virulent opposition of the whites in the Wallowa removed any chance of giving up land to the Nez Perce. Without hope, Joseph died on the Colville Reservation on September 21, 1904; it was said that he died of a broken heart.

According to the Canadian North-West Mounted Police, ninety-eight warriors and about two hundred women and children managed to escape to Canada, joining Sitting Bull's camp for a while. While many Nez Perce eventually returned to the reservations, White Bird adamantly refused to leave Canada. He was killed in 1892 by a twenty-six-year-old Nez Perce man called Nez Perce Sam who blamed White Bird, who was also a medicine man, for the deaths of his children. According to Indian custom, if a patient dies, one can hold the medicine man accountable. Nez Perce Sam received a life sentence for the crime but starved himself to death within the year.[127]

The tragedy of the Nez Perce is epic. In three months, 750 to 800 men, women and children traveled 1,700 miles over some of the most difficult terrain in America, outfighting, outmarching and outwitting the US Army, only to be stopped 40 miles from safety. They killed about 180 people, mostly soldiers, and wounded another 150, while losing about 120 of their own, mostly women and children.[128]

Their just cause, unity, courage, endurance and tenacity was for naught. In the battle of cultures, there can be only one winner.

CHAPTER 11

# THE LAST YEARS

The year 1878 witnessed fewer combat operations against the Indians. The most serious in western Montana took place in July, when Lieutenant Thomas Wallace and a detachment of thirteen soldiers of the 3rd Infantry and several civilian guides were sent from Fort Missoula to apprehend a band of marauding Nez Perce. These Indians had recrossed the border from Canada to return to their homeland in Idaho. On their way home, they stole some horses and killed some white men in Rock Creek, about twenty-five miles from Missoula. Lieutenant Wallace overtook and surprised the Nez Perce along the Clearwater River in Idaho and, in a two-hour engagement, killed six, wounded three and captured thirty-one while suffering no casualties.[129]

As the Indian threat lessened, army life once again returned to routine. Soldiers drilled, maintained and repaired buildings and roads, constructed telegraph lines and escorted Indian hunting parties to eastern Montana. Yet there was still the occasional difficulty with individual or small bands of Indians, such as in August 1879, when Lieutenant Colonel Chipman, commander at Fort Missoula, wrote to the Indian agent, Peter Ronan, to report drunken Indians in the Missoula vicinity who were molesting the citizens. Ronan was instructed to make sure the Indians returned to the reservation. A year later, the commander complained of Indians looting gardens and orchards around Missoula.[130] There was also a minor conflict outside Fort Logan at the head of White's Gulch. Later, a small band of Bannocks fled from the Idaho Territory, where they had been on the warpath. This latter threat was quickly met by Colonel Miles with his usual efficiency, as he closed in on the hostiles at Clark's Fork Pass leading into the Yellowstone basin. Eleven warriors were killed and a large number wounded, and the entire camp was captured.

The one remaining concern was Sitting Bull and the Sioux still living in Canada. With difficulties dealing with their own indigenous people, the Canadians were reluctant hosts to the Sioux, but peaceful relations were maintained. An American correspondent, invited to the Sioux reserve, reported nearly 1,100 lodges, 2,500 warriors and plenty of guns and ammunition but little food. Closely watched by the Northwest Mounted Police, the Sioux still managed to occasionally cross the border in small bands to hunt in Montana. In each instance, the army was ready. In April 1879, an entire band of hostile Sioux was caught and killed on Careless Creek in the Musselshell River Valley. Later that summer, settlers clashed with another band of Indians on Sixteen Mile Creek and killed all but one. Time was running out for the Indians—the plains were rapidly being settled, there were more whites, the army was now experienced and ready to act and communication had improved with more telegraph lines connecting the far-flung settlements and forts.

In the summer of 1879, it was learned that Sitting Bull had moved south of the border to the Milk River. Colonel Miles again responded quickly and massively. The Sioux swiftly retreated, leaving much of their buffalo meat and supplies behind. With meat in short supply and with the buffalo herds disappearing rapidly, the end was drawing near.

During the winter of 1879–80, small bands of Sioux crossed the border but were always chased back; occasionally some were captured. A raid on the Fort Custer military reservation in April 1880 netted the Sioux fifty horses, but they were pursued for over one hundred miles and captured. Colonel Miles informed Sitting Bull that the captured warriors would be held until they all surrendered. A delegation of 8 Sioux soon arrived at Fort Keogh to discuss surrender terms, and eventually 2,000 Sioux surrendered. In November 1880, Miles was promoted to brigadier general and left to take command of the Department of the Columbia. On April 11, 1881, at Fort Buford in the Dakota Territory, Chief Low Dog surrendered with 185 men, women and children. Then finally, on July 19, 1881, Sitting Bull with the remaining 187 Sioux left Canada and surrendered. With the exception of continuing problems with the Apaches in the American Southwest, the Indian Wars were over.[131]

Meanwhile, by the summer of 1878, Colonel Gibbon and the 7th Infantry had been transferred out of the District of Montana, although post records from Fort Shaw show that Captain Rawn was still there as late as October 1878, when he went on leave and eventually appeared before the Army Retiring Board in April 1879. After the board's refusal to retire him on medical grounds, Rawn rejoined his regiment at Fort Snelling, Minnesota, where post records show that he stayed until June 1880. Fort Snelling was located at the confluence of the Minnesota and Mississippi Rivers. Established in 1819, it was sold to developers in 1857, used by the state during the Civil War and transferred back to the army in 1866, when it became the headquarters and supply base for the Department of Dakota.[132]

Post returns next place Captain Rawn at Fort Stevenson, Dakota Territory, from June 1880 until December 1883. Fort Stevenson was established in 1867 above the mouth of the Knife River to provide protection against the Sioux, keep the Missouri River open and protect the mail.[133] In June 1883, the garrison was transferred to Fort Buford, Dakota Territory, and in August of that year, the post was transferred to the Fort Berthold Indian Agency. During this time, Rawn was stationed for several months at a time at Fort Laramie and Fort Fred Steele, in the Wyoming Territory; Camp Loder, Montana Territory; and Fort Supply, Indian Territory. Frequently, Rawn would be acting commander in Gibbon's absences.

On April 18, 1884, Charles Rawn was promoted to major in the 24th Infantry, one of four regiments of African Americans—or "Buffalo Soldiers," as the Indians called them—created after the Civil War. He formally signed his oath of office at Fort Laramie on May 16 and proceeded to Texas for what would be his last duty station.

Fort Elliott was established in February 1875 in the Texas Panhandle on the North Fork of the Red River and then moved a short distance to the headwaters of Sweetwater Creek in June 1875. Although there were few Indians in the immediate area, the fort was created to keep the Indians on their reservations and to monitor Indian hunting parties. The nearest telegraph was 146 miles away at Fort Sill; the nearest railroad was 184 miles away in Dodge, Kansas; and headquarters of the 24th Infantry was 92 miles east at Fort Supply. The surrounding country is a rolling prairie, with plenty of water and sufficient timber. As fort commander, Major Rawn lived in an eight-room house with his wife and three children (a fourth, Isabel, was born at Fort Elliott in 1885). There was a small library and school, and Rawn, perhaps under the urging of his wife, added a stage and seating to the schoolhouse for concerts and theatrical productions.[134]

Major Rawn was a good fit for the command. Having served in New Mexico during the Civil War, he was familiar with the territory, and he had

PAGE EIGHT

**From FAMILY ALBUMS of HARRISBURG**

**THE LATE MAJ. CHARLES COATESWORTH RAWN**

A son of the late Charles Coatesworth Pinkney Rawn and Frances Peacock Clendenin, of this city, Major Rawn served most of his mature life in the United States Army. He entered the service soon after his graduation from Princeton. Fighting against the Indians in the West under General Custer, Major Rawn was cited for bravery in the Little Big Horn engagement. He married Miss Isabel Nauman, of Lancaster. They are survived by a daughter, Miss Margaret Rawn, of Lancaster. Major Rawn was an uncle of Mrs. Carl W. Davis, of River road, near Rockville.

*Right*: A studio photograph of Major Charles C. Rawn; no date, taken from his obituary in 1887. *Courtesy Historical Society of Dauphin County, Harrisburg, Pennsylvania.*

*Below*: Fort Stevenson, Dakota Territory, was built in 1867 and abandoned in 1883; it is shown here circa 1885. *Courtesy the State Historical Society of North Dakota.*

Fort Elliott, Texas, was established in 1875 and served until 1890; it is shown here circa 1880. *Courtesy Texas State Library and Archives Commission.*

Officers at Fort Elliott, circa 1880. *Courtesy Texas State Library and Archives Commission.*

served with bravery and honor as captain for almost twenty years. One imagines that, given his love and respect for his father and his reasons for joining the army, to command free black Americans provided him with a great sense of satisfaction and fulfillment. Given his history of illness—which was getting worse, requiring sick leave for months at a time since 1876—it is possible that he was given a promotion to an easy and low-prestige position as a longtime career soldier approaching the end of that career.

Rawn's health did not improve. He had been granted a six-month sick leave while at Fort Stevenson because of a stomach ulcer, chronic hepatitis and mental hallucinations and another four-month leave while at Fort Laramie. After two years at Fort Elliott, on June 10, 1886, he requested a five-month sick leave and permission to leave the limits of the division. He enclosed a medical certificate signed by R.C. Newton, post surgeon, stating:

> *I have carefully examined this officer, and find that he's suffering from sciatica and chronic muscular and arthritic rheumatism affecting principally the lower limbs and knee and toe joints. This officer has been of bilious temperament during the two years I have known him at this post, and has constantly been obliged to take cathartic medicine. This torpidity of the liver*

The 23rd Infantry at Fort Elliott, circa 1880. *Courtesy Texas State Library and Archives Commission.*

> *dates back, in my opinion to Major Rawn's service in Florida some years ago where he contracted chronic malarial toxaemia. For the last two months he has been troubled with his personal complaint, which has so far proved unamenable to treatment except palliation, although it is only for ten days that he has been so completely laid up as to go upon the sick report. From considerable experience with similar cases, I do not hesitate to declare my opinion that several months* [sic] *residence upon the Atlantic seaboard, or at least until cold weather, will be necessary to restore Major Rawn to health.*

Sick leave was granted, and when the five months were coming to a close in October, Dr. Oliver Roland, Rawn's personal physician in Lancaster, Pennsylvania, wrote in support of an extension and confirmed that "he is suffering from sciatica, and chronic muscular and arthritic rheumatism. His case is further complicated by a torpid or sluggish action of the liver, evidently the result of chronic malarial poisoning." He concluded that "Major Rawn in his present physical condition is not, in justice to himself or the best interests of the service, fitted to perform military duty."

Requests for continued extension of sick leave were regularly repeated and approved. However, on April 2, 1887, Rawn was finally ordered to report back to duty. Dr. Roland immediately protested, stating that "if my judgement is not deemed sufficient I merit an additional examination. I have just left this man's bedside and common justice demands that I enter my protest against his removal in his present condition." Rawn's brother-in-law and local political power, George Nauman, wrote to the authorities:

> *My brother-in-law, Maj. C.C. Rawn, U.S.A. has been for some time on sick leave. His leave of absence has expired and his application for an extension has been refused by the War Department, and he has been ordered back to his post. His physical condition is such that he is really unfit to return to duty and he has forwarded Dr. Roland's certificate to that effect. If you can aid him in any way, you will greatly oblige me.*

This appeal eventually reached the desk of Lieutenant General Sherman, along with a reminder of the distinguished career of Rawn's father-in-law, Colonel George Nauman. Sherman ordered the medical officer nearest Lancaster to proceed there and make a report.

Attending Surgeon Colonel David Magruder of Philadelphia was dispatched on April 14 to review the case. He found Rawn suffering from chronic malarial poisoning and a greatly enlarged liver. He reported that

Lancaster Cemetery, Lancaster, Pennsylvania. *Author's photograph.*

both eyes were deeply jaundiced and during his paroxysms there was a great sluggishness of the brain with a nonviolence closely bordering on coma. The coordination of the muscular movement of his lower extremities was so imperfect that locomotion was labored and uncertain, and the serious trouble in the spinal cord was due to spasmodic contractions in the legs. Dr. Magruder reported that Major Rawn was "totally unfit" for any duty and recommended a sick leave extension of six months but doubted if he would ever return. The extension was granted on April 18.

At 4:00 a.m. on October 6, 1887, Major Charles Rawn died.[135]

The *Harrisburg Patriot* reported on Friday, October 7, with some hyperbole and a certain lack of historical accuracy regarding his role in the Nez Perce War:

> *Major Charles C. Rawn, a veteran of the war and distinguished officer in the United States Army died at his residence in Lancaster yesterday morning after an illness of a painful character which lasted over a year... While on the frontier engaged in numerous Indian campaigns, Major Rawn won considerable renown for bravery. In Montana, with General Gibbons* [sic], *during the Nez Perces war, he pursued, held in check and finally captured*

The graves of Major Charles C. Rawn and his wife, Isabel. *Author's photograph.*

> *the famous Chief Joseph, holding him until the main body of troops came up, and thus put an end to the war. For his gallantry on this occasion he was highly complimented by General Gibbons* [sic]. *Deceased was a genial, courteous gentleman, held in high regard by all who knew him.*

Major Charles Coatesworth Rawn died just before his fiftieth birthday. We can easily understand how a man with his upbringing joined the Union forces in the Civil War. We can also easily understand how, through familial influence, he rose through the ranks and avoided most of the serious battles of that war. It is harder to understand why a man of such pedigree and education chose to continue to serve in the army. Was it the comradery? Was it a sense of duty? Was it that he found his role in life? We will probably never know.

However, we can make certain assumptions about his career. Like most officers, he probably admired the Indians, and from his father, we can suspect there was a certain amount of empathy toward them; but he had a job to do. One would like to believe that it was Captain Rawn telling his men not to shoot at the women at the Big Hole. It is interesting that after the Nez Perce War, he actively sought medical discharge from the army for an injury suffered years before and was disappointed when the Army Retiring Board turned down his request. We can see a man, an ordinary man, doing what he thought best, surviving as best he could, loving his wife and raising his children in the harsh environment of the frontier army. We may not agree with Sergeant Charles Loynes when he stated that "a better officer never lived," but we have to respect that enlisted man's opinion.

# NOTES

## *Chapter 1*

1. Afrolumens Project, "Charles Coatesworth Pinkney Rawn," 4.
2. Ibid., 5.

## *Chapter 2*

3. Rawn, Military Service Files, Historical Museum at Fort Missoula, and Big Hole National Battlefield.
4. McManus, *American Courage*, 168.
5. Ibid.

## *Chapter 3*

6. Utley, *Frontier Regulars*, 12.
7. Ibid., 13.
8. Ibid., 14.
9. Ibid., 22.
10. Ibid., 14–15.
11. Ibid., 15–16.
12. Smith, *Dose of Frontier Soldiering*, 62.
13. Utley, *Frontier Regulars*, 20–25.

14. Ibid., 36–49.
15. McChristian, *U.S. Army in the West*, 3–246.
16. Utley, *Frontier Regulars*, 71–78; Agnew, *Life of a Soldier*, 59–80.
17. McManus, *American Courage*, 69.
18. Agnew, *Life of a Soldier*, 140.
19. Ibid., 144–50.
20. Ibid., 151–58.
21. Ibid., 190.
22. Pond, "Masonry in North Dakota"; Rawn, *Rawn Journals*.
23. Agnew, *Life of a Soldier*, 172–73.
24. Nevin, *Soldiers*, 73.
25. Delo, *Peddlers and Post Traders*, 47–185.
26. Rockwell, *U.S. Army in Frontier Montana*, 234.
27. "Fort Shaw," Montana Historical Society.
28. Roe, *Army Letters*, 89.
29. Rawn, Military Service Files.
30. "Portrait and Biographical Record," 295–97.
31. Rawn, Military Service Files.
32. Eales, *Army Wives*, 1–21.
33. Ibid., 33.
34. Ibid., 38–62.
35. Roe, *Army Letters*, 123–24.
36. Eales, *Army Wives*, 95–107.
37. Stallard, *Glittering Misery*, 75–99.
38. Rockwell, *U.S. Army in Frontier Montana*, 109.

## *Chapter 4*

39. Smith, *Dose of Frontier Soldiering*, 80.
40. Utley, *Indian Frontier*, 86–93.
41. Brown, *Fetterman Massacre*, 11–229.
42. Agnew, *Life of a Soldier*, 210–14.
43. Utley, *Frontier Regulars*, 199.
44. Fifer, *Montana Battlefields*, 35.
45. Ibid., 31–39; Rockwell, *U.S. Army in Frontier Montana*, 161–220; Utley, *Frontier Regulars*, 198.
46. Eckroth and Hagen, *Baker's Battle*, 28.
47. Lubetkin, "Forgotten Yellowstone Surveying Expeditions," 39.

48. Eckroth and Hagen, *Baker's Battle*, 33–34.
49. Lubetkin, "'No Fighting Is to Be Apprehended,'" 29–35.
50. Bradley, *March of the Montana Column*, 57–58.
51. Eckroth and Hagen, *Baker's Battle*, 37–40.
52. Ibid., 42.
53. Lubetkin, "'No Fighting Is to Be Apprehended,'" 35.
54. Fifer, *Montana Battlefields*, 44.
55. Bradley, *March of the Montana Column*, 60.
56. Eckroth and Hagen, *Baker's Battle*, 44.
57. Ibid., 43–52.
58. Ibid., 54–55; Lubetkin, "'No Fighting Is to Be Apprehended,'" 36–37.
59. Eckroth and Hagen, *Baker's Battle*, 60–63, 72–73; Lubetkin, "'No Fighting Is to Be Apprehended,'" 34–41; Rockwell, *U.S. Army in Frontier Montana*, 249.
60. Bradley, *March of the Montana Column*, 63.
61. Lubetkin, "'No Fighting Is to Be Apprehended,'" 41.

## *Chapter 5*

62. Agnew, *Life of a Soldier*, 14.
63. Ibid., 21–35.
64. Fifer, *Montana Battlefields*, 61–69.
65. Bradley, *March of the Montana Column*, 13.
66. Ibid., 14.
67. Fifer, *Montana Battlefields*, 69–90.
68. Ibid., 93–125; Utley, *Frontier Regulars*, 263–69.
69. Fifer, *Montana Battlefields*, 125.
70. Bradley, *March of the Montana Column*, 173–74.
71. Fifer, *Montana Battlefields*, 131–55.

## *Chapter 6*

72. Koelbel with Cohen, *Missoula*, 19–44.
73. Blades and Wike, "Fort Missoula," 29–30.
74. Schulmeyer, "Presenting the Men."
75. "Rawn," Big Hole National Battlefield.
76. Rothermich, "Historical Reprints."

77. Loynes, "Nez Perce War," 267.
78. Glynn, *That Beautiful Little Post*, 7.
79. Rawn, "September 30, 1877, Letter to Assistant Adjutant General."
80. Rawn, "Letterbook," July 13, 1877 entry.
81. Rawn, "September 30, 1877, Letter to Assistant Adjutant General."
82. Flaherty, "History of Fort Missoula," 5.
83. Sheridan and Sherman, "Inspection Made in the Summer of 1877," 41–44.
84. Flaherty, "History of Fort Missoula," 5.

## *Chapter 7*

85. Josephy, *Nez Perce Indians*, xv–xix; Pearson, *Nez Perces in the Indian Territory*, 1–9.
86. McDermott, *Forlorn Hope*, xiii; Pearson, *Nez Perces in the Indian Territory*, 4–11.
87. Boatner, *Civil War Dictionary*, 413–14.
88. Pearson, *Nez Perces in the Indian Territory*, 14–27; Josephy, *Nez Perce Indians*, 485–508.
89. Highberger, *Death of Wind Blowing*, 36.
90. Joseph, *That All People May Be One People*, 22.
91. Ibid., 25.
92. Fifer, *Montana Battlefields*, 163.
93. Glynn, *That Beautiful Little Post*, 9–10; Bob Painter, *White Bird*, 19–65; Josephy, *Nez Perce Indians*, 509–63; Josephy, *Nez Perce Country*, 111–25.

## *Chapter 8*

94. Josephy, *Nez Perce Country*, 125.
95. Rockwell, *U.S. Army in Frontier Montana*, 424.
96. Rawn, "Letterbook," July 16 entry.
97. Ibid.
98. Rawn, "September 30, 1877, Letter to Assistant Adjutant General."
99. Rawn, "Letterbook," July 25 entry.
100. Gordon, *When Money Grew on Trees*, 70.
101. Rawn, "September 30, 1877, Letter to Assistant Adjutant General."
102. Josephy, *Nez Perce Indians*, 566–69.

103. Rawn, "Letterbook," July 27 entry.
104. Rawn, "September 30, 1877, Letter to Assistant Adjutant General."
105. Josephy, *Nez Perce Indians*, 570.
106. Rawn, "September 30, 1877, Letter to Assistant Adjutant General."
107. Ibid.
108. Howard, *Saga of Chief Joseph*, 233.
109. McWhorter, *Yellow Wolf*, 107.
110. Josephy, *Nez Perce Indians*, 571–72.
111. Historical Museum at Fort Missoula Research Files, Boxes 9–12; Glynn, *That Beautiful Little Post*, 16.
112. Rawn, Military Service Files.
113. Brown, *Flight of the Nez Perce*, 228.
114. Loynes, "Nez Perce War," 267.

## Chapter 9

115. Josephy, *Nez Perce Indians*, 573–78.
116. McWhorter, *Yellow Wolf*, 108.
117. Ibid., 109.
118. Loynes, "Nez Perce War," 269.
119. Ibid., 271.
120. Ibid., 273.
121. McManus, *American Courage*, 190–206; Haines, *Elusive Victory*, 42–162; Brown, *Flight of the Nez Perce*, 236–70; Glynn, *That Beautiful Little Post*, 18–23.
122. Rawn, "Letterbook," September–November entries.
123. Rawn, "September 30, 1877, Letter to Assistant Adjutant General."

## Chapter 10

124. Josephy, *Nez Perce Indians*, 590
125. McWhorter, *Yellow Wolf*, 211.
126. Wood, *Pursuit & Capture of Chief Joseph*, 29.
127. Greene, *Beyond Bear's Paw*, 47–163.
128. Utley, *Frontier Regulars*, 316–24; Wood, *Pursuit & Capture of Chief Joseph*, 12–31; O'Neal, *Nez Perce Exile*, 11–40; Painter, *White Bird*, 82–91; Gulick, *Chief Joseph Country*, 241–60; Wooster, *Nelson Miles*, 96–110; Rockwell,

*U.S. Army in Frontier Montana*, 452–73; Fifer, *Montana Battlefields*, 182–214; Pearson, *Nez Perces in the Indian Territory*, 52–293; Bond, *Flatboating on the Yellowstone*, 11–45; Brown, *Flight of the Nez Perce*, 268–431.

## *Chapter 11*

129. Glynn, *That Beautiful Little Post*, 39–40; Porter, "History of the Fort Missoula Cemetery."
130. Glynn, *That Beautiful Little Post*, 40.
131. Rockwell, *U.S. Army in Frontier Montana*, 474–83.
132. Roberts, *Encyclopedia of Historic Forts*, 438.
133. Ibid., 633.
134. Ibid., 762.
135. Rawn, Military Service Files.

# BIBLIOGRAPHY


Afrolumens Project, Central Pennsylvania African American History for Everyone. "Harrisburg Cemetery African American History Perspectives: Charles Coatesworth Pinckney Rawn." http://afrolumens.org. 2003–04.

Agnew, Jeremy. *Life of a Soldier on the Western Frontier*. Missoula, MT: Mountain Press Publishing Company, 2008.

Blades, Thomas E., and John W. Wike. "Fort Missoula." *Military Affairs* 13, no. 1 (Spring 1949).

Boatner, Mark Mayo, II. *The Civil War Dictionary*. New York: David McKay Company, Inc., 1959.

Bond, Fred G. *Flatboating on the Yellowstone, 1877*. Staten Island, NY: Ward Hill Press, 1998.

Bradley, Lieutenant James H. *The March of the Montana Column, A Prelude to the Custer Disaster*. Edited by Edgar I. Stewart. Norman: University of Oklahoma Press, 1961.

Brady, Cyrus Townsend. *Indian Fights and Fighters*. Lincoln: University of Nebraska Press, 1971.

Brown, Dee. *The Fetterman Massacre*. Lincoln: University of Nebraska Press, 1962.

Brown, Mark. *The Flight of the Nez Perce*. Lincoln: University of Nebraska Press, 1967.

Buecker, Thomas R. *A Brave Soldier & Honest Gentleman: Lt. James E.H. Foster in the West, 1873–1881*. Lincoln: Nebraska State Historical Society Books, 2013.

Craighill, William P. *The Army Officer's Pocket Companion; Principally Designed for Staff Officers in the Field*. New York: D. Van Nostrand, 1862.

Delo, David M. *Peddlers and Post Traders: The Army Sutler on the Frontier*. Helena, MT: Kingfisher Books, 1998.

Eales, Anne Bruner. *Army Wives on the American Frontier: Living by the Bugles*. Boulder, CO: Johnson Books, 1996.

Eckroth, David, and Harold Hagen. *Baker's Battle on the Yellowstone, August 14, 1872*. Sheridan, WY: Frontier Heritage Alliance, 2004.

Fifer, Barbara. *Montana Battlefields, 1806–1877: Native Americans and the U.S. Army at War*. Helena, MT: Farcountry Press, 2005.

Flaherty, Stacy. "History of Fort Missoula." Historical Museum at Fort Missoula Research Files, Missoula, MT, Box 9.

"Fort Shaw." Montana Historical Society Manuscript Files, Helena, MT.

Glynn, Gary. *That Beautiful Little Post: The Story of Fort Missoula*. Missoula, MT: Friends of the Historical Museum at Fort Missoula and Big Elk Books, 2013.

Gordon, Greg. *When Money Grew on Trees: A.B. Hammond and the Age of the Timber Barons*. Norman: University of Oklahoma Press, 2014.

Greene, Jerome A. *Beyond Bear's Paw: The Nez Perce Indians in Canada*. Norman: University of Oklahoma Press, 2010.

———, comp. and ed. *Indian War Veterans: Memories of Army Life and Campaigns in the West, 1864–1898*. New York: Savas Beatie, LLC, 2007.

Griffin, Dr. Dustin, comp. *Biographical Outline of Charles Cotesworth Rawn (1837–1887)*. N.p., 2005.

Gulick, Bill. *Chief Joseph Country: Land of the Nez Perce*. Caldwell, ID: Caxton Printers, Ltd., 1994.

Haines, Aubrey L. *An Elusive Victory: The Battle of the Big Hole*. Helena, MT: Falcon Publishing, 1991.

Highberger, Mark. *The Death of Wind Blowing: The Story of the 1876 Murder that Helped Trigger the Nez Perce War*. Wallowa, OR: Bear Creek Press, 2000.

Howard, Helen Addison. *Saga of Chief Joseph*. Lincoln: University of Nebraska Press, 1941.

Joseph, Chief. *That All People May Be One People, Send Rain to Wash the Face of the Earth*. Kooskia, ID: Mountain Meadow Press, 1995.

Josephy, Alvin M., Jr. *Nez Perce Country*. Lincoln: University of Nebraska Press, 2007.

———. *The Nez Perce Indians and the Opening of the Northwest*. Boston: Houghton Mifflin Company, 1965.

Koelbel, Leonora, with Stan Cohen. *Missoula, the Way It Was: A Portrait of an Early Western Town*. Missoula, MT: Pictorial Histories Publishing Co., Inc., 2014.

Loynes, Charles N. "The Nez Perce War and the Battle of the Big Hole." In *Indian War Veterans: Memories of Army Life and Campaigns in the West, 1864–1898*. Compiled and edited by Jerome A. Greene. New York: Savas Beatie, LLC, 2007.

Lubetkin, M. John. "The Forgotten Yellowstone Surveying Expeditions of 1871: W. Milnor Roberts and the Northern Pacific Railroad in Montana." *Montana, The Magazine of Western History* (Winter 2002).

———. "'No Fighting Is to Be Apprehended': Major Eugene Baker, Sitting Bull & The Northern Pacific Railroad's 1872 Western Yellowstone Surveying Expedition." *Montana, The Magazine of Western History* (Summer 2006).

McChristian, Douglas C. *The U.S. Army in the West, 1870–1880; Uniforms, Weapons, and Equipment*. Norman: University of Nebraska Press, 1995.

McDermott, John D. *Forlorn Hope: The Nez Perce Victory at White Bird Canyon*. Caldwell, ID: Caxton Press, 2003.

McManus, John C. *American Courage, American Carnage: 7th Infantry Chronicles*. New York: Tom Doherty Associates Book, 2009.

McWhorter, L.V. *Yellow Wolf: His Own Story*. Caldwell, ID: Caxton Press, 2008.

"Memorial of the Legislature of Montana Territory to 43rd Congress, February 5, 1874." Historical Museum at Fort Missoula Research Files, Missoula, MT, Box 11.

Montana Historical Society Photograph Files, Helena, MT.

Nevin, David. *The Soldiers*. New York: Time-Life Books, 1973.

O'Neal, Larry D. *Nez Perce Exile: The Struggle for Freedom, 1877–1885*. Wallowa, OR: Bear Creek Press, 2006.

Painter, Bob. *White Bird: The Last Great Warrior Chief of the Nez Perce*. Fairfield, WA: Ye Galleon Press, 2002.

Pearson, J. Diane. *The Nez Perces in the Indian Territory: Nimiipuu Survival*. Norman: University of Oklahoma Press, 2008.

Pond, Harold Sackett, PGM. "Masonry in North Dakota." www.ndmasons.com.

Porter, Marcia. "History of the Fort Missoula Cemetery: Stories in Stones." Historical Museum at Fort Missoula Research Files, Missoula, MT.

"Portrait and Biographical Record of Lancaster County Pennsylvania." Google Books, 2015.

"Rawn." Big Hole National Battlefield Research Files, Wisdom, MT.

Rawn, Captain Charles C. "Letterbook, Fort Missoula, Montana, 1877." Historical Museum at Fort Missoula Collections Library, Missoula, MT.

———. "September 30, 1877, Letter to Assistant Adjutant General, Department of Dakota, St. Paul, Minn." Historical Museum at Fort Missoula, Missoula, MT, Research Files, Box 9.

"Rawn, Charles Coatesworth, Military Service Files." Big Hole National Battlefield Research Files, Wisdom, MT.

"Rawn, Charles Coatesworth, Military Service Files." Historical Museum at Fort Missoula Research Files, Missoula, MT, Boxes 9–11.

Rawn, Charles Coatesworth Pinckney. *The Rawn Journals, 1830–1865.* Historical Society of Dauphin County, Harrisburg, PA.

Roberts, Robert B. *Encyclopedia of Historic Forts: The Military, Pioneer, and Trading Posts of the United States*. New York: MacMillan Publishing Company, 1988.

Rockwell, Ronald V. *The U.S. Army in Frontier Montana.* Helena, MT: Sweetgrass Books, 2009.

Roe, Frances Marie Antoinette Mack. *Army Letters from an Officer's Wife, 1871–1888.* San Francisco: Editora Griffo, 2015.

Ross, Rickard A. *First to Arrive on Custer's Battlefield with the Montana Column: Frederick E. Server, Montana Pioneer, Soldier, and Explorer*. El Segundo, CA: Upton and Sons, Publishers, 2010.

Rothermich, Captain A.E., ed. "Historical Reprints, Early Days at Fort Missoula." *Sources of Northwest History* 23, Missoula, MT: Montana State University; *Frontier and Midland, A Magazine of the Northwest*, Missoula, MT: Montana State University 16, no. 3 (Spring 1936).

Schulmeyer, A.C. "Presenting the Men of Companies 'A' and 'I,' 7th U.S. Infantry in August, 1877." Big Hole National Battlefield Research Paper, Summer 1978, Historical Museum at Fort Missoula Research Files, Missoula, MT, Box 10.

Sheridan, General P.H., and General W.T. Sherman. "Inspection Made in the Summer of 1877." Washington, D.C.: Government Printing Office, 1878, Historical Museum at Fort Missoula Research Files, Missoula, MT, Box 10.

Smith, Thomas T. *A Dose of Frontier Soldiering: The Memoirs of Corporal E.A. Bude, Frontier Regular Infantry, 1877–1882*. Lincoln: University of Nebraska Press, 1994.

Stallard, Patricia Y. *Glittering Misery: Dependents of the Indian-Fighting Army*. Norman: University of Oklahoma Press, 1978.

Utley, Robert M. *Frontier Regulars: The United States Army and the Indian, 1866–1891*. New York: MacMillan Publishing Co., Inc., 1973.

———. *The Indian Frontier of the American West, 1846–1890*. Albuquerque: University of New Mexico Press, 1984.

*Weekly Missoulian*, June 22–September 7, 1877.

Wood, Charles Erskine Scott. *The Pursuit & Capture of Chief Joseph: A Story of the End of the Nez Perce War*. Wallowa, OR: Bear Creek Press, 2006.

Wooster, Robert. *Nelson Miles & the Twilight of the Frontier Army*. Lincoln: University of Nebraska Press, 1993.

# INDEX

## D



## E



## F



## G



## H



## J



## L



## M

## N



## O



## P



## R



## S



## T



## U



## W

# ABOUT THE FOREWORD AUTHOR

Gary Glynn served on the board of the Friends of the Historical Museum at Fort Missoula from 1995 to 2001 and on the Missoula County Board of Trustees for the Historical Museum from 2001 to 2010. He received the Lt. James Moss Award for outstanding service to the museum in 2011. He has been writing about military history, Montana history and Fort Missoula for over thirty years. Recent works include *Montana's Home Front During World War II*, 2$^{nd}$ ed. (Big Elk Books, 2011), *Historic Photos of Montana* (Turner Publishing, 2009) and *That Beautiful Little Post: The Story of Fort Missoula* (Friends of the Historical Museum at Fort Missoula and Big Elk Books, 2013). He is currently working on the *Brink of War*, the story of the United States' intervention during the Mexican Revolution.

# ABOUT THE AUTHOR

Dr. Robert Munro Brown was the executive director at the Historical Museum at Fort Missoula from 1991 until his retirement in 2014. He received his BA from Ursinus College in 1973, MA from Rivier College in 1978 and PhD from the University of New Hampshire in 1983. He has been active in the museum community, serving as a board member for the American Association for State and Local History, peer reviewer for the American Alliance of Museums, board member and officer of the Mountain-Plains Museums Association and board member and president of the Museums Association of Montana. He does first-person presentations as Captain Rawn and Christopher P. Higgins, founder of Missoula.

www.ingramcontent.com/pod-product-compliance
Lightning Source LLC
LaVergne TN
LVHW010946100826
845153LV00002B/150

* 9 7 8 1 5 3 1 6 9 8 7 5 1 *